EARNING AND SPENDING

EARNING & SPENDING

BY

E. E. REYNOLDS

Author of *Ourselves and the Community*

'He showed me a very excellent argument,
to prove, that our importing less than we
export do not impoverish the Kingdom,
according to the received opinion; which,
though it be a paradox, and that I do not
remember the argument, yet methought
there was a great deal in what he said.'

SAMUEL PEPYS, *Diary,* 29 Feb., 1663/4

CAMBRIDGE
AT THE UNIVERSITY PRESS
1951

CAMBRIDGE UNIVERSITY PRESS
Cambridge, New York, Melbourne, Madrid, Cape Town,
Singapore, São Paulo, Delhi, Tokyo, Mexico City

Cambridge University Press
The Edinburgh Building, Cambridge CB2 8RU, UK

Published in the United States of America by Cambridge University Press, New York

www.cambridge.org
Information on this title: www.cambridge.org/9781107614154

First published 1951
First paperback edition 2011

A catalogue record for this publication is available from the British Library

ISBN 978-1-107-61415-4 Paperback

CONTENTS

LIST OF DIAGRAMS AND MAPS		vi
INTRODUCTION		vii
CHAPTER I	Population	I
2	Occupations	14
3	The Trade Unions	27
4	Employers and Employed	37
5	The Organisation of Industry	45
6	The State in Industry	57
7	Distribution	66
8	Money	77
9	External Trade	90
INDEX		100

DIAGRAMS AND MAPS

I	Growth of Population	2
II	Birth and Death Rates	3
III	Changing Balance of Population	5
IV	Distribution of Population, 1700 and 1800	9
V	Movements of Population	10
VI	Occupations, 1949-1950	16
VII	Average Weekly Earnings	22
VIII	Cost of Living, 1914-1946	23
IX	Membership of Trade Unions	31
X	Main Foods, 1949	68
XI	Purchasing Power of Pound, 1938-1950	82
XII	External Trade and Unemployment, 1924-38	84

(Diagram III is reproduced by permission of the
Controller, His Majesty's Stationery Office. It
is taken from *The British Way and Purpose*, 1944,
p. 387)

INTRODUCTION

THIS book is an introductory description of our national economy; it does not attempt to expound economic theories, but aims at providing a sound foundation on which further study can be reliably based.

The plan and method are related to those local and social studies which are being increasingly carried out in our schools.[1] This book should be useful at the stage when the local studies need to be co-ordinated with national studies, and discussion can fruitfully begin. The age-group in mind is that of 'young persons'—defined for legal purposes as 'over fourteen and under seventeen years of age'.

METHOD OF STUDY. While an individual reader can well follow the suggestions in this book, the most productive plan would be for a group of readers (with not more than six members) to follow the course under the supervision of an adult. The members can then pool their information when they come together and proceed to discuss the problems that arise from their inquiries.

INQUIRY. At the end of each chapter will be found a number of subjects for inquiry and discussion. These are not intended to cover the whole field; other subjects will suggest themselves in the course of study and the leader will be able to propose others.

The phrase 'your own locality' is frequently used; this must be interpreted according to local conditions. Thus in a big industrial city, one ward may be sufficient for some

---

[1] See the Ministry of Education pamphlet, *Citizens Growing Up*, and, for an example of the first stage of inquiry, another of the Ministry's pamphlets, *Local Studies: Bishop Auckland*.

inquiries; in a country district, a parish may be the best area for study. If practicable, it is best to choose an area that is already defined for official purposes; official statistics of population, and so on, are more likely to be available. It is, however, most important that inquiries should not be limited to the neighbourhood; the town-dweller needs to go out into the surrounding country, and a town group might profitably have a second centre in a village. Similarly, the country-dweller needs to get into direct touch with an industrial centre. It would be most advantageous if a town group and a country group could be linked up and occasionally have joint meetings.

The leader will make sure that the members of his group understand the need for keeping accurate records always marked with the source of information. A common method of making records is helpful.

DISCUSSION. Discussions should be conducted under the usual debating rules so that time is not wasted on desultory argument; where possible a definite proposition should be put forward; this should not be too limited in its scope. It does not matter if no firm conclusion is reached. The value of the discussion lies in the presentation of several points of view and in the stimulus to thought that results. The leader should stress the importance of basing opinions on verifiable evidence (collected previously by inquiry, or accessible at the meeting in official reports, etc.). In this way the habit of intelligent consideration of problems can be developed. It is not necessary to point out what a valuable contribution this is to the training of citizens.

Each member should write a report of each discussion to include a record of the information that has been produced and of the various views expressed. This is a very important part of the method of study.

SOURCES OF INFORMATION. The personal inquiries made by the members of the groups will seldom cover the whole field, and may be very limited in their scope owing to the nature of the locality. They must be supplemented from other sources, and national information must of necessity be gained from official reports. Part of the training should be devoted to learning where information can be obtained, the degree of authority it has, and how it can be used.

The local newspaper should be studied regularly and cuttings extracted and filed that relate to the subjects of inquiry. Industrialists, managers, Trade Union officials, managers of Employment Exchanges, town clerks, and so on, are usually glad to give information if they are approached in the spirit of genuine inquiry rather than from curiosity or from a political party point of view. At this stage it is most desirable that all inquiries and discussions should be free from party political advocacy. The librarian ot the local public library is usually eager to help with advice on reports and books that may be of use.

For inquiries that go beyond local interests, it is necessary to watch the national newspapers and to turn also to official publications. One member of a group might well be given the task of making cuttings from a daily newspaper; the best plan would be for several different newspapers to be studied by the group, each member being responsible for one newspaper.

In searching for material it is well first of all to find out if anything relevant is published by His Majesty's Stationery Office. The scope of its publications is very wide and the range of subjects considerable. A visit to one of its sales departments is the quickest way of seeing what is available, but those who live away from these few centres,[1]

[1]London, Edinburgh, Manchester, Cardiff, Bristol, Belfast.

should write to the Controller, H.M.S.O., York House, Kingsway, London, W.C.2. Some days may pass before a reply is received.

Three publications are particularly useful :

Annual Abstract of Statistics. (10s.) This is an indispensable source of statistics about population, employment, trade, etc. Each page will suggest topics for discussion.

Board of Trade Journal. (Weekly 6d.) This gives the latest available figures for trade, and often contains informative articles on many aspects of industry.

Ministry of Labour Gazette. (Monthly 9d.) As the name suggests, this gives information on employment, wages, etc.

These three publications should be available in the local public library; if they are not, a request should be made to the librarian.

A useful general reference book is *Whitaker's Almanack.* It is published in two editions: the Shorter Edition omits the information on foreign countries given in the Complete Edition. The 1950 edition of *Chambers' Encyclopædia* will be found useful for reference on many topics and for statistics.

A book of this kind can give statistics only up to the latest date before going to press. One of the routine tasks of the reader, or group, should be to add later statistics as they are published and extend the diagrams accordingly. All statistics given here are from official sources.

This book deals with one branch of social studies; it must not be considered in isolation but must be related to other subjects—history, geography, and so on. It has not been possible in this short book to give more than an occasional historical note, or to refer to a few general books that throw light on some of the topics. It is hoped that this need for linking one study with another will be kept in mind by the leader and the reader.

Earning and Spending may be regarded as a junior companion to my book *Ourselves and the Community*, which deals with central and local government, the structure of the Commonwealth and Empire, and international organisation.

I am most grateful to Professor E. A. G. Robinson for having read through my manuscript and for the most helpful suggestions he made for its improvement.

OCTOBER, 1950   E. E. R.

POPULATION

It was not until 1801 that a census (an official numbering) of the population of Great Britain was made. This gave a total of 9,178,980 persons living in England and Wales, and 1,608,420 in Scotland. The census of 1931 gave 39,952,377 for England and Wales, and 4,842,980 for Scotland. Thus in the course of one hundred and thirty years the population of the whole country was more than quadrupled.

There are no reliable figures for the population before 1801. Estimates have been made which put the total for England during the twelfth century at about one and a half million; by the beginning of the sixteenth century this number had doubled, and by 1700 it had again doubled to a total of a little under six millions. For six centuries after the Norman Conquest the increase in population was gradual; then it began to go upwards rapidly. Diagram I shows the growth of population from 1811.

What were the causes of this increase since 1700 ? There were many influences at work to reduce the dangers of disease and to make people more healthy. Towns were being paved and drained, and piped water made available; refuse was removed; greater variety of fresh food in winter was possible with the introduction of root crops ; personal cleanliness was made easier by the supply of cheaper soap and of cotton underwear. Such factors had far more effect on general health than the rather slow progress in medical knowledge, but hospitals became more efficient and increased in number. What a long way the people of the eighteenth and early nineteenth centuries had still to go is well shown in the novels of Charles Dickens, where the conditions of town life at the beginning of Queen Victoria's reign are vividly described.

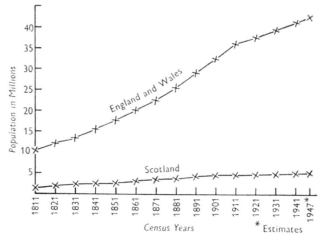

Diagram I—Growth of Population

The history of one family living in London during the eighteenth century shows the improvement in health. William Mawhood (1682-1757) was a woollen-draper who lived next to the gatehouse of St. Bartholomew-the-Great in Smithfield. His wife had twelve children; nine of them died in infancy. It was the youngest child, also named William (1724-1797) who inherited his father's business and lived with his family in the same house. His wife had eight children, only two of whom died in infancy; of the others, one lived to be seventy-nine and another to be eighty-five.

2

BIRTH AND DEATH RATES. This decline in the number of infants dying (infantile mortality) is one reason why the number of adults increased during the nineteenth century. The general death rate (the number of people who die each year out of every thousand of the population) has also declined steadily; it was affected to some extent during the two world wars. There has also been a decline in the birth rate. Diagram II gives curves for both rates. If these two curves come very close together, as in 1940, there is little

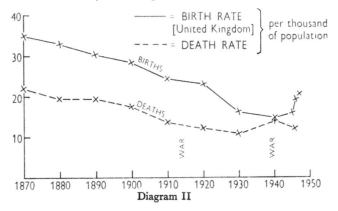

Diagram II

change in the size of the population; should the death rate exceed the birth rate (as it did in 1730), then the population decreases. During the period following the outbreak of war in 1939 there was an increase in the birth rate; this was due to special causes and may not therefore be maintained.

One reason for the decline in the birth rate since 1870 has been that people prefer to have small families so that they can enjoy a better standard of living. A typical family of 1860 had five or more children. For example,

3

Lord Baden-Powell, who was born in 1857, had six brothers and three sisters. The typical family of today has two children. There are many explanations for this change: higher standards of care and education are now accepted than were thought necessary a hundred years ago; children are no longer allowed to go to work to add a few shillings to the family income; there are far more ways of enjoying leisure—and most people have more leisure now; these mean spending money that at one time went in maintaining the family.

One result of the decline in both the birth and the death rate is that the population is getting older. Have you, for instance, ever noticed at what ages some of the Kings of England died? Edward IV at 41; Henry VII at 53; Henry VIII at 56; James I at 59; Charles II at 55. As we read our history we think of them dying as old men, and in their day they were so considered. Today a man of fifty-five years of age has a reasonable expectation of at least another twenty years of life. The enormous strides in the science of medicine and more widely spread knowledge of how to keep healthy (not the least of which concerns our meals) have made a great difference to the length of life. Thus in 1851, out of a thousand people, forty-seven would be over sixty-five years of age; today that figure would be more than doubled to over a hundred.

Diagram III shows how the relative sizes of three main age-groups changed between 1911 and 1931. At the bottom is a forecast of what the position may be in 1971; this must not be taken too seriously, as in dealing with human beings it is unsafe to predict how they will behave. We are not symbols fitted neatly into rectangles. It is, however, clear that in future the number of old people will increase compared with those of working age. But what do we mean by 'old people'? The definition changes from generation to generation. People last longer (if they are not killed on the roads or in a war), but their working life can also last longer if they have the opportunities.

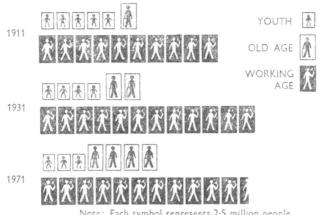

Note: Each symbol represents 2·5 million people

Diagram III—Changing Balance of Population
From BWP (H.M.S.O.), p. 387

DENSITY OF POPULATION. A more important aspect of this subject of population is the relation between the size of a country and the number of people in it. This is called the density of population, and is usually given as so many people to the square mile—assuming they were evenly spread out. Here are the figures for some countries:

	To the sq. mile			To the sq. mile
England & Wales	750		Europe (average, excl.	
Belgium	714		U.S.S.R.)	212
Holland	713			
Germany (pre-war)	480		U.S.A.	47
France	190		New Zealand	17·3
Scotland	172		Canada	3·5
			Australia	2·5

In comparing such figures we must take into account the nature of each country; thus Canada has ice-bound regions, and Australia has vast deserts. It would be a fairer comparison to put the Canadian figure at 9, and the Australian at 4·5.

The figure for England alone (leaving out Wales) would be just over 800 persons to the square mile, making it the most densely populated country in the world. You can see at once what a problem this raises in food supply alone.

There has been much discussion as to whether our great population is an advantage or a disadvantage. Such arguments can have no practical result unless we are prepared to 'liquidate' a portion of the population. Some see a solution of this problem of overcrowding in emigration to such under-populated lands as Canada and Australia. But those countries do not want old people or those who do not suit their industrial and commercial requirements. Few people (in comparison with the larger number needed to make a real difference in population) want to leave their native land or even their home towns. Compulsory emigration is out of the question in a free country.

Here are the numbers of British emigrants to some countries during 1948 and 1949:

	1948	1949
Canada	34,487	20,762
Australia	34,445	53,059
New Zealand	6,927	9,261
S. Africa & S. Rhodesia	32,232	15,283
Other British Countries	21,224	21,672
U.S.A.	19,600	16,237

These are not substantial numbers in comparison with our total population.

DISTRIBUTION OF POPULATION. When we talk of the density of the population we are imagining a situation that does not exist; one of the great difficulties in using statistics is that they suggest an artificial condition of living. We are not spread out evenly all over the country. Actually over eighty per cent of the people in England and Wales live in towns. A third of them are concentrated in half a dozen great cities.

Of the five million population of Scotland over two-fifths live either in Lanark (Glasgow) or Midlothian (Edinburgh).

An aeroplane view of England at the beginning of the eighteenth century would have shown a country that was mainly agricultural and well wooded; even the few big towns would have seemed partly hidden by the trees of gardens and orchards. By contrast we are now striving to save the few open spaces left to us amidst the hotch-potch of streets. That vanished England was a land of cultivators and craftsmen, for much of the making of things was done in villages and cottages and not in factories. The large towns were trading and business centres and ports. The areas of greatest density of population were in the south and the east of the country.

A change became noticeable in the second half of the eighteenth century; the name 'Industrial Revolution' has been given to this development of great industrial towns with highly concentrated populations; the balance between urban and rural was radically altered.

The word 'Revolution' makes us think of some sudden, even violent, break in history, but this was a silent revolution and happened without any scheme of change. It was not entirely industrial, for there were important developments in agriculture going on at the same time—new methods of production, new crops, enclosures of waste land, and so on. In industry the greatest and decisive development was in the invention and the use of machinery;

7

this meant many people working together in factories instead of in their own homes or in small workshops in the towns and villages. Unfortunately this also meant the too rapid growth of manufacturing centres in the Midlands, in Lancashire, in the West Riding and on Tyneside and in South Wales. Not enough thought was given to the housing, health and happiness of the many thousands of men, women and children who took up this new kind of employment or were born amidst such dreadful conditions.[1] The effect on the distribution of the population was considerable. The centres of industry were near the coal-fields which supplied the necessary power for the machine age. Whereas the main concentration of population had previously been south of a line drawn between Bristol and Hull, it now settled north of that line. This change is shown in the pair of maps in Diagram IV. These also show the general increase in population over most of the country.

During our century another shifting of population has taken place, and is still progressing. Industry is no longer so dependent on being near the coal-fields; electricity has become the main source of power and can be distributed all over the country. New factories can be built wherever suitable land and transport are available. There are many new 'light' industries, as they are called—such as the making of radio sets or of objects from plastics. These can be carried on away from the old industrial regions with their prison-like buildings, slag-heaps and slums. They also make it possible to find fresh employment in areas where old industries, such as coal-mining or ship-building, have

[1]Benjamin Disraeli's *Sybil* (1845), Charles Kingsley's *Alton Locke* (1850) and *Yeast* (1851), and Mrs. Gaskell's *Mary Barton* (1848) and *North and South* (1855) help us to understand the social conditions of the first half of the last century.

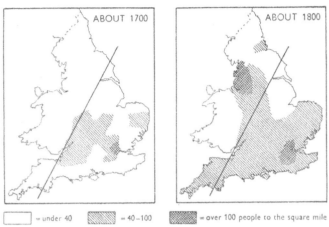

Diagram IV—Distribution of Population

declined, or do not now need so many workers owing to more efficient methods. Some of the hardest hit of these areas are now being helped under a Government scheme of assistance in building and equipping the necessary factories.

Diagram V shows the areas of greatest density of population at the present time and the tendency to move towards London and the south-east. Only an absolute government could control such movements of the population; all that can be done is to increase the opportunities for employment in the less popular areas in the hope that young people will remain there and not join the trek south-eastwards.

CLASSES. Another way of studying the subject of population is to consider what are usually called the classes into which it is grouped. For purposes of description it is sometimes convenient to talk of upper, middle and lower

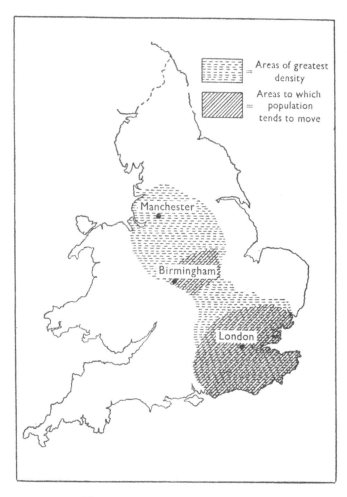

Diagram V—Movements of Population

classes; but we also talk of the 'professional class', and even of the 'criminal class'. It is clear that the word 'class' can be used in several ways. When the 'class warfare' is mentioned by extremists, we get yet another point of view.

It is an interesting fact that social class groupings have never been maintained rigidly in this country; there has always been movement from class to class or from social grade to social grade, and we have fortunately escaped the evil effects of a parasitic aristocracy that, for example, could only be broken in eighteenth-century France by a violent Revolution. The younger sons of the English aristocracy have entered the Church, or the Army, or the Navy, but they have also gone into trade and have sailed across the seas to develop new settlements. There has also been a steady recruitment of the peerage or of the landed gentry from trade and from the Services. During the nineteenth century wealth was often the stepping-stone (and a slippery one) to a baronetcy or barony. This fluidity in our social structure is a saving factor in national life. Nor is it without significance that such terms as 'rentier', 'bourgeois' and 'proletariat' are not our native words. We need not take too seriously occasional displays of snobbishness that offend our sense of justice. Respect for tradition has helped to give us stability, and we can give deference to rank and authority without loss of self-respect.

We have referred to the Industrial Revolution which marked the century following 1750; it may be that future generations will call ours the century of the Social Revolution. A silent transformation is being worked out in the structure of society. It is not the result of any preconceived plan. The extremes of wealth and poverty have almost gone; property (a basis for class distinction) is no longer the mark of a relatively small section of the population, since more and more people become owners of their houses (for example, through Building Societies); a man or woman with technical knowledge and organising ability has the chance of reaching a position of great responsibility; the Services and professions are no longer the preserves of one group. These and many similar changes are breaking down distinctions recognised by former generations. This present-day revolution has been summed up in the paradox, 'There is no longer a middle class, because we are now all middle class.'

In the next chapter we must consider another classification of the population—by the kind of employment.

Subjects for inquiry and discussion

1. Why has the population of Scotland not increased appreciably during this century?
2. Find out the average size of a family in your locality from at least twenty families of varying types.
3. What are the advantages and disadvantages of being the only child in a family?
4. Will the greater facilities for free education, the health services and family allowances encourage larger families?
5. What is the effect on national welfare of an increasing number of old people?
6. Find out from at least twenty people of different ages what they consider to be the beginning of old age.
7. What provision in your locality is there for caring for lonely old people? Can you suggest improvements?
8. What special problems arise in countries like England and Belgium where there is a high density of population?

9. Can you suggest ways in which such high densities could be reduced ?
10. Would it be an advantage if the population of this country declined in numbers ?
11. Study a map showing density of population in Europe. Try to explain the variations from country to country.
12. Collect population, birth and death figures for your locality. What changes have there been during the past hundred years ? Can you explain these ?
13. If you were starting a factory for producing an electrical appliance, where would you select the site? Give reasons for your choice.
14. What are the advantages and disadvantages of living in a village ?
15. Suggest ways in which country people could be persuaded to remain in the country.
16. To what social class or classes do you and your friends belong ?

CHAPTER 2

OCCUPATIONS

THE whole of this book could be filled with a list of the kinds of employment followed in our country.

Distinctions between ways of earning a living have long been recognised in our common speech, but the application of the words has changed from time to time. Thus Dr. Johnson stated in his Dictionary (1755) that 'the term *profession* is particularly used of divinity, physick and law.' Today we should extend this meaning to include such occupations as teaching, consultant engineering, analytical chemistry and other sciences, accountancy, art, and architecture. Nor is it easy to say what distinguishes such professions from other forms of employment; they all call for specialised training and most of them can only be entered after qualification by examination, but many other kinds of employment also necessitate training and the attainment of a required standard of efficiency.

Another distinction is between skilled and unskilled work. Here again it is difficult to draw a hard and fast line; all labour involves some skill even if it is just the right handling of a shovel; the degree of skill needed to qualify as a skilled labourer defies description.

We also have the use of such words as 'fee', 'salary', and 'wages' as another kind of difference between kinds of work.

Many of these differences are not economic but social, and may depend on how one speaks, or dresses, or behaves, or to the kind of education one has had. The man who

14

earns his living in a profession may well receive less money than one who is engaged in an occupation that does not carry with it any social prestige.

Another distinction is made when we speak of a 'black-coated' or 'white-collar' worker, and the implication is that this is socially superior to being a man who does physical labour. Even in one kind of trade such distinctions have been made; thus, a bricklayer always wore a bowler hat at work ! These and other differences tend to disappear; we all dress much alike, and all work has its social value.

A more useful classification for our purposes would be by three large groups:

1. *Production:* farming, mining, engineering, etc.
2. *Distribution:* retail trade, transport, etc.
3. *Services:* schools, hospitals, banks, etc.

This scheme emphasises the part an occupation plays in the national economy. By 'economy' is here meant the management of the resources of the country, just as the economy of a family is the way in which the parents decide the income shall be spent. In a State, some people (the producers) are engaged in growing crops for food or tending animals to give us milk and meat, or in making (manufacturing) things we need; others (the distributors) are busy selling things or moving them to places where they are wanted; while others—a more miscellaneous group—are occupied in teaching us, or caring for our health, or providing us with amusement. This very broad classification does not tell us much about the different occupations. So we need something more detailed if we are to get a clear idea of the situation.

Diagram **VI** is based on an official classification. We can see at once how one group compares in size with the

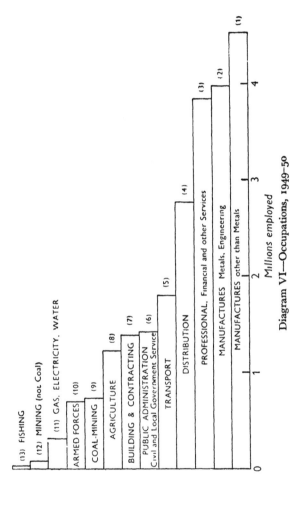

Diagram VI—Occupations, 1949–50

others. You will notice that two groups (1 and 2) are labelled 'manufactures'; the difference is based on the raw material used—metal. The combined size of these two groups shows us how important a part manufactures have in our economy.

Group 3 is made up of those services mentioned above. We can all appreciate the service rendered by a doctor, but the typist and the bank clerk share in the useful work of organising our resources. So too the distributive trades (4) have an important function as links between producer and consumer. The only other groups on which comment may be useful are 6 and 8. The growth of the Civil Service[1] and other forms of administrative employment is a characteristic of our times. The whole-time staff of the Civil Service totalled 348,900 in 1938; ten years later it was 673,400. This rapid increase is an indication of the extension of the work of the Government. Whether this is good or bad, necessary or extravagant, cannot be discussed here. The point to note is that this group now exceeds group 8— agriculture. The smallness of our country and the density of the population make it difficult to expand our agriculture; many problems would be solved if we could grow much more of our food, but our inability to increase this production very much is a fact we have to take into account when studying the country's resources. Our position may be compared with that of France, where over a third of the working population is occupied in agriculture.

GETTING A JOB. How do people get jobs ? The question 'What do you want to be ?' is not always an easy one to answer. Some boys and girls make up their minds definitely; others have a general notion that, for instance, they

---

[1]The term Civil Service is here used to cover all those employed by the State and not merely clerical workers.

would prefer to work out-of-doors rather than at a desk. Those who want to enter one of the professions have a well-marked route to follow of training and examination. More and more occupations call for some kind of qualification by examination; some, for instance, expect the applicant to have passed a recognised public examination before beginning the specialised training for the job. The Ministry of Labour publishes a series of pamphlets, *Choice of Careers*, which are helpful in giving information and also in suggesting possibilities in a great variety of occupations.

An apprenticeship is sometimes required. In former times a seven years' apprenticeship was necessary before anyone could practise a craft or trade. This system was developed by the trade gilds that were established in the Middle Ages and succeeding centuries. This strict rule was done away with in 1834, when greater freedom of occupation was allowed. Today each trade decides its own conditions of employment whether by apprenticeship or by some other system of qualification. Some of the professions have a scheme on the lines of an apprenticeship, using such terms as 'articled clerk' and 'pupil' instead of apprentice.

This ancient practice must not be confused with the travesty of it described in *Oliver Twist* (see chapter 3). Parish or Poor Law apprentices were destitute children handed over, for a consideration, to an employer who would take them nominally for training in a trade or craft. This was little better than a form of slavery in spite of its legal safeguards.

Many people are content to accept whatever opening comes their way; they are not ambitious and have no desire for positions of responsibility. Provided the job gives them a living wage and the chance to bring up a family they are satisfied, even if the work may be of a routine or monotonous kind. Some prefer hard physical labour. It is as well that we vary so widely in our abilities and needs, for there is much dull and even disagreeable work to be done. A small, very small, proportion of the population evades work and lives on its wits. They may be professional burglars, or speculators, or what are now called 'spivs'. Their goings-on provide news, so we may tend to think there are more of them than in fact they number.

FIXING WAGES. How are wages fixed? For the most part they are now paid according to agreements reached through discussion and negotiation between employers and representatives of the employed. More will be said of this in considering the function of the Trade Unions. There are, however, trades and occupations where it is difficult to organise a negotiating body because the workers are scattered in small units and cannot easily come together. To meet such cases Parliament has passed Acts to regulate wages.

There is nothing new in this statutory (i.e. by Act of Parliament) regulation of wages. In the fourteenth century, when a dearth of labour followed the Black Death, a statute was passed to keep wages at what they had been before the pestilence, but this and later attempts to keep wages down did not succeed. Then there was the important Statute of Artificers (1563); the purpose was 'to yield unto the hired person, both in time of plenty and in time of scarcity, a convenient proportion of wages.' The Justices of the Peace were given the task of deciding rates, and, as most of them were interested employers, they tended to keep wages as low as possible. They continued to make regulations up to the period of the Industrial Revolution.

Modern wage regulation, as we understand it, by the State begins in 1909 with the passing of the Trades Boards Act. This was the outcome of rising indignation at the conditions in 'sweated' trades, that is, occupations, often carried on at home, where the pay was scandalously low for the amount of time given to the work. Thomas Hood's poem 'The Song of the Shirt' (published in *Punch* at Christmas, 1843) drew attention to this evil more than half a century before effective action was taken.

> ' Work — work — work !
> My labour never flags;
> And what are its wages ? A bed of straw,
> A crust of bread — and rags.'

When that was written it was not considered to be the business of the State to interfere (as it was termed) between employer and worker. The Act of 1909 set up Trade Boards to fix minimum wages in such industries as Paper Box Making, Ready-made Tailoring, and Chain Making. The same method was later extended to cover other kinds of work, and in 1945 the Trade Boards were re-named Wages Councils and the Minister of Labour was given power to set up a Wage Council in any industry where there is no satisfactory scheme for settling wages. Other Acts to regulate wages are the Agricultural Wages Acts of 1924 and 1940, the Road Haulage Act of 1938, and the Catering Wages Act of 1943. The Holidays with Pay Act of 1938 may also be considered as one of the ways in which wages in certain industries are regulated by the Government; by this employers in trades subject to wage regulation by law have to provide holidays with pay for their workers. Many other industries have adopted the same principle voluntarily.

CALCULATING WAGES. There are several methods of calculating wages. In the professions (apart from those where fees are customary) an annual salary is the rule; this rises according to length of service and with increasing responsibility. Weekly wages are based on an agreed number of working hours per week. In 1947 the average numbers of hours worked in the most important industries was forty-five. Overtime (i.e. hours additional to the agreed weekly number) is paid at a higher rate. Thus time and a quarter means the usual rate per hour plus a quarter of that rate. For example, if the rate is 2s. per hour, overtime is paid at 2s. 6d. an hour. Sometimes the rate is time and a half, or even double. Some workers engaged on difficult work or using specialised tools may get a higher rate than others in the same factory. A higher rate is also paid for night work, or for Sundays, or for work on public holidays.

The standard rate may be expressed as so much an hour, or per shift, or per week of so many hours. A shift is the continuous period a worker does at one stretch. Another system of payment is by piece-work; by this the worker is paid so much for each unit of production for which he is responsible, with a minimum sum as a basis; higher output then means higher earnings. Piece-work payment is not regarded favourably by many workers; they usually prefer a wage based on time with higher rates for overtime and special days.

This description covers most of the methods of calculating wages, but there are others, such as various bonus systems to encourage individual effort; there is payment to a gang or team of a lump sum for a job, the money then being divided amongst the members according to an agreed scheme. Yet another modification is that of the sliding scale; by this wages are adjusted according to the rise or fall in the cost of living. Diagram VII shows the average weekly earnings in selected occupations.

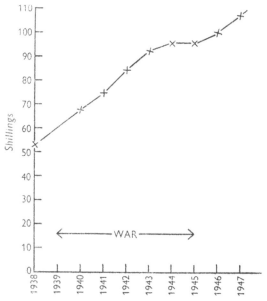

Diagram VII—Average Weekly Earnings in certain Industries (in shillings)

COST OF LIVING. The figure or index number for the cost of living is arrived at by calculating the prices that have to be paid for food, rent, clothing, and so on. By taking one year as the standard and calling this 100, it is possible to compare one year with another. For instance if 1914 is taken as 100, the index figure for 1944 is 201, which means that living was twice as expensive in 1944 as in 1914 (when sweets were four ounces a penny and tobacco six-pence an ounce). If we take 1939 at 100, then 1944 is 130, showing that the cost of living had gone up by a third. A sliding scale for wages takes these figures into account, and if the rise is above an agreed figure, wages go up in industries where the scheme is in force. The method is not so popular when there is a fall in the cost-of-living index !

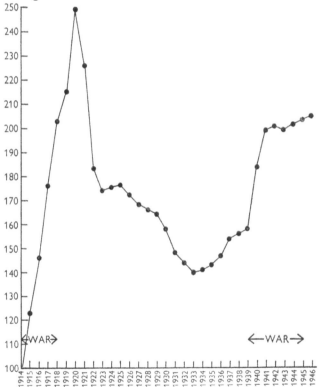

Diagram VIII—Cost of Living, *Ministry of Labour Index, July 1914 = 100*

23

Diagram VIII (p. 23) shows the cost-of-living curve for the period 1914 to 1946, taking 1914 as 100. The Ministry of Labour changed the method of calculating the index figure in 1947.

DEDUCTIONS. Some deductions are made when salaries or wages are paid. Those liable to income tax have a proportion of the tax deducted by the employer, who pays the total for all his employees to the Collector of Taxes. This system is known as PAYE ('pay as you earn') and the individual is saved the trouble of sending in his tax separately in two half-yearly sums; the Collector of Taxes is also saved the trouble of dunning defaulters.

Other deductions are for National Insurance (Health, Unemployment, Retirement, etc.). The employer also pays a share and the State adds a further sum. The following are the rates for employed persons.

Description of employed person	Weekly rate of contribution.	
	Initial rate. From Oct. 1946	Permanent rate. From Oct. 1951
	s. d.	s. d.
Men between the ages of 18 and 70 (not including men over the age of 65 who have retired from regular employment):		
Earning remuneration at a weekly rate exceeding 30s.	4 7	4 9
Earning remuneration at a weekly rate of 30s. or less	2 8	2 9
Women between the ages of 18 and 65 (not including women over the age of 60 who have retired from regular employment):		
Earning remuneration at a weekly rate exceeding 30s.	3 7	3 9
Earning remuneration at a weekly rate of 30s. or less	2 2	2 3
Boys under the age of 18	2 8	2 9
Girls under the age of 18	2 2	2 3

Here we need only concern ourselves with unemployment benefit. The basic weekly rate of payment is 26s. There are additions for children and other dependents. Payment is made for 180 week-days, if the unemployed man or woman is out of work for as long as that; if still unemployed when that period expires, he or she can have the case considered by a local tribunal, with the possibility of an extension of benefit.

In 1909 Labour Exchanges (now called Employment Exchanges) were established to help employers find men and to help men find work. Previously to 1909 a man out of work just tramped round asking for a job unless he was lucky enough to hear of one being vacant. During the 1930s (see Diagram XII, p. 84) the Labour Exchanges were thronged with men out of work; they drew their unemployment money as long as the scheme allowed, after which they were helped by Public Assistance; there was a serious shortage of work at that time and this caused much unhappiness. The period following the Second World War was one of full employment, and it is to be hoped that the experiences of the 1930s will never be repeated. Perhaps the most serious effect of prolonged unemployment on the individual is that he feels that he has no part to play in the life of the community—he is not wanted. This saps a man's self-respect and cannot but have a bad effect on the spirit of the people as a whole.

Subjects for inquiry and discussion

1. Arrange the following under the headings of Production, Distribution, and Services:

    lawyer, farm worker, accountant, motor mechanic, baker, dustman, teacher, bus conductor, clergyman, coal miner, ironmonger, jockey.

2. In your locality, *either* make a list of the chief industries, *or* show on a map how the land on a farm is used.

3. Make a list of the kinds of shops in the main street of a town. Is there any advantage in having more than one shop of the same kind?

4. What kind of occupation would you like to follow? What are the reasons for your choice?

5. Ask six of your friends, *either* what they want to be, *or* why they have taken their present jobs.

6. Are there any arrangements in your locality for giving advice on careers? What kind of advice do you think is most useful?

7. What industries in your locality have apprenticeship schemes? Find out the terms of the indentures.

8. Do you think it better to learn a trade or craft by experience in the workshop, or to have preliminary theoretical training with some practice?

9. Should wages vary according to the rise or fall in the cost of living? Suggest a suitable scheme for a sliding scale of this kind for a local industry.

10. Which do you think is the fairest method of calculating wages, by time or piece-work? Find out how wages are calculated in your locality in three industries.

11. What are the rates for overtime and special days in two industries in your locality?

12. Ask six of your friends who are at work if they like the PAYE scheme. Summarise their arguments for and against.

CHAPTER 3

THE TRADE UNIONS

REFERENCE was made in the last chapter to the part played by Trade Unions in making agreements with the employers. Since the Unions are so important in the industrial organisation of the country, we must consider their history and work in greater detail.

A Trade Union is defined in the Oxford English Dictionary as 'an association of the workers in any trade or in allied trades for the protection and furtherance of their interests in regard to wages, hours, and conditions of labour and for the provision, from their common funds, of pecuniary assistance to the members during strikes, unemployment, old age, etc.' The need for sickness, unemployment and old age benefits has now been largely superseded by the National Health and Insurance schemes.

A distinction should be made (though it is not always easy to make it) between a Trade Union, as usually understood, and a professional organisation such as the British Medical Association. Such a body is primarily concerned with establishing and maintaining standards of qualification for recognition as a member, and with creating a code of professional conduct; it does, however, also concern itself with scales of fees and salaries. Perhaps membership of the Trades Union Congress (see below p. 34) may be taken as a working distinction.

HISTORY. Three main stages in the development of Trades Unions may be recognised:

1. Establishing the right to combine.
2. Establishing the right to strike.
3. Establishing the right to be consulted.

The order of these is important as it explains much in the attitude of the Unions towards labour problems. The legacy of hard and bitter struggles is not quickly spent, and suspicions linger long after the original causes are dead.

1. *The right to combine.*

While industry was carried on in small units in towns and villages there was no possibility, nor so much need, for nation-wide associations to protect the workers. The Industrial Revolution combined with the effects of prolonged war (1793-1815) resulted in much distress and misery. The greater concentration of labour meant easier conditions for getting together and discussing grievances. It was in the spirit of the times that Parliament passed two Acts (1799 and 1800) to prohibit what were called Combinations—that is, associations of people for taking common action. One of the purposes named as illegal was any attempt to raise wages. The Acts had an appearance of fairness since employers were liable to prosecution as well as workers, but no prosecution of an employer is on record. There are, however, many against workers. One example must suffice.

When a soldier, William Temple, returned from the Peninsular War he became a spinner near Manchester. He and some of his fellows decided to ask for a small increase in wages; the employer refused and the men left his factory. Thereupon the employer passed the word round to other factory owners, who refused to employ these men. Temple consulted a lawyer and raised a subscription to prosecute the first employer. For this, Temple and several others were arrested and charged with 'conspiracy to raise wages and control their masters'. As he could not find the heavy bail demanded, he was kept in prison for five months until his trial. He and four of his fellows were arraigned for 'conspiring, confederating, combining, and agreeing for the price of their labour'. Temple was sentenced to a further twelve months imprisonment, and when he came out it took him another year before he could find employment.

Such stories could be multiplied and lists given of far harder sentences. It was out of such sufferings that the Trade Union movement was born.

Combinations were regarded as conspiracies against the nation and as likely to lead to political action. The workers found a number of ways of getting round the laws; the most successful was the Friendly Society, the purpose of which was to help the members in times of distress and illness. Though these Societies did not take direct action in question of wages—had they done so they would at once have been suppressed—they had another effect not less important for the future. They were self-governing and in their local meetings the members learned how to manage their affairs in an orderly manner ; they appointed their officers and discussed any problems that arose. Thus they were, unconsciously, training themselves in democratic methods of conducting business. This laid a sound foundation for the development of the Unions as soon as they were permitted to come out into the open.

The Combination Laws Repeal Act of 1824 and the Amendment Act of 1825 permitted the formation of associations for improving conditions of labour. A number of hampering conditions were laid down, but Trade Unions began to be formed and to increase in numbers. Old ideas still persisted; thus in 1834 some farm workers at Tolpuddle in Dorset were transported for imposing an oath of secrecy on the members of their Union.

2. *The right to strike.*

The Trade Union Act of 1871 recognised the Unions and the right to strike, but severe penalties were imposed for intimidation. A series of Acts from 1875 to 1913 removed some restrictions and, as a result of cases submitted to law, defined more clearly the status of the Unions and their powers over their funds.

The General Strike of 1926 produced an Act in 1927 that was greatly resented by the Unions as it seemed vindictive. Restrictions were placed on sympathetic strikes, and it was made necessary for a member to declare if he wanted to contribute to the political fund of his Union; previously he could 'contract out', that is, to say he did not want to contribute. This Act was repealed in 1946.

3. *The right of consultation.*

During the 1914-1918 War the Government found it best to consult the Unions before making regulations affecting industrial labour. This was a successful policy and prevented much trouble. The War of 1939-1945 again showed the value of such consultations, and the economic problems after the war made it desirable to continue that policy. The fact that a Labour Government came into office in 1945 no doubt increased the amount of such consultation, but any other Government would probably have found it a wise policy to follow. The Unions are also sometimes represented on Royal Commissions and other public inquiries, and submit evidence on matters concerning labour and social legislation.

MEMBERSHIP. Diagram IX shows how the Union membership has fluctuated since 1890. The earliest figure available is for 1868, when the number was 118,367, but this was probably below the actual membership.

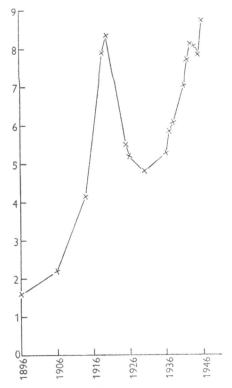

Diagram IX—Membership of Trade Unions (in millions)

Several attempts were made in the first part of the nineteenth century to form one national all-inclusive Union; there was, for example, the Grand National Consolidated

Trades Union of 1833, and the National Association of Trade Unions of 1845. Such attempts were too ambitious at a time when only a small proportion of the workers were organised. Had such a project been achieved, a most dangerous situation might have arisen, since one section of the population could have held the rest to ransom. The natural line of development was for men doing the same kind of work to unite; thus one factory may contain members of several Unions. These Craft Unions, as they may be called, consist of skilled workers. Later the need was felt for Unions with a wider basis and some of the smaller ones joined together and extended their membership to include all workers—skilled and unskilled—in an industry. This policy may be dated from 1851, when the Amalgamated Society of Engineers was established. This Union is now absorbed in the Amalgamated Engineering Union. So we get two movements: a decline in the number of Unions but an increase in the total membership.

In 1936 there were 1,036 Unions in the United Kingdom with a membership of 5,295,000; ten years later there were 753 Unions having a total of 8,714,000 members.

This decrease in the number of Unions is not all gain. The larger a Union, the less do the ordinary members feel in touch with the chief officials. This is a cause of discontent owing to the loss of direct personal contacts. The problem cannot be easily solved; the larger Union, such as the Transport and General Workers with over a million members, is in a stronger bargaining position than a small union.

Functions. The main purpose of a Trade Union is to protect, and if possible improve, the wages and conditions of labour of its members. This is done chiefly through negotiations with employers. During the periods of serious unemployment the Unions have tried to spread the work available by laying down rules as to the amount of work to be done in a given period: for example, the number of bricks to be laid in an hour. They have also insisted that each worker should be confined to the job for which he is employed: for example, that a carpenter should not do a plumbing job of which he may be capable.

The outsider is sometimes irritated at these restrictive practices, as they are called, and thinks some of them unreasonable (as some may be) and cannot understand the point of view of the Unions. If, however, we realise that such practices are the outcome of the struggle for decent conditions and fair terms of labour, we shall be more sympathetic. At the back of the minds of many workers is the dread of unemployment, and the bitter experiences of the 1930s are not easily forgotten. With better understanding between employers and workers (the growth of which will be described later) and the abundance of work, such restrictions on output call for revision.

The Unions have also given much attention to the conditions under which their members work; these include such matters as healthy factory buildings, safety precautions, provisions for canteens, and so on. This purpose is achieved by promoting, or by supporting proposals for, legislation to safeguard the worker in the mine or factory from injury or from unhealthy conditions. Some have established their own convalescent homes and made provision for holiday centres.

ORGANISATION. The Unions vary in their ways of running their affairs. There is usually an annual conference to which delegates are sent from the local branches; the conference may have power to make or change rules of membership, but in some Unions such proposals have to be submitted to a national ballot. The executive committee sometimes has considerable powers of action between conference meetings, but some Unions prefer to have all important proposals confirmed, or rejected, by the local branches. These again vary in constitution; some are based on districts to include all members living in such areas, while others are formed of members in one factory or firm. Shop stewards are appointed to watch the interests of the Union members in workshops or factory departments. These representatives have an important part to play in securing smooth working, as they can bring to the notice of the management any problems or difficulties or grievances that might, if ignored, lead to serious trouble.

One of the most contentious aspects of Trade Unionism is that of the 'closed shop'—that is, a demand that all workers in a factory or business shall be members of the appropriate Unions. The justification for this is that all workers have benefited from the activities of the Unions by getting better wages and conditions, and therefore all should be members. Policy in this question varies amongst the Unions. Some employers have attempted to enforce the opposite rule—that is, to employ only non-union men. Most employers today realise that good working relations are more easily obtained if the Unions are regarded not as natural enemies, but as useful allies.

TRADES UNION CONGRESS. The work of the Trade Unions is co-ordinated by the Trades Union Congress (founded 1868); this supplies the place of the earlier dream of a Grand National all-inclusive Union. Nearly all Unions are members of the Congress, but some, such

34

as the National Union of Teachers, remain outside. Each Union retains its separate identity and the control of its own policy; the Congress does not give orders to its member Unions; it is a consultative and advisory body. It meets annually for the discussion of general principles and of matters of common interest. Naturally the Unions give great weight to its suggestions, but they are not bound by these. In between the annual meetings a General Council keeps watch over affairs.

One sign of the importance of the Unions and of the Congress is the increasing practice of consultation between them and the Government. This not only keeps the Government aware of the trend of opinion in the Unions, but the Unions themselves get a wider view of affairs and of their own responsibilities.

EMPLOYERS' ASSOCIATIONS. The employers also have their associations. Some of these are for the promotion of trade and production, such as the Motor Trade Association or the Federation of British Industries. Here we are concerned with associations whose main purpose is negotiation with the Trade Unions. An example is the Engineering and Allied Employers' National Federation. Such a body can carry out discussions with the Unions as representing the employers in an industry. There is also the British Employers' Confederation, which may be regarded as the counterpart of the Trades Union Congress.

It would be a mistake to think of these organisations of employers and workers as solely concerned with hard bargaining about wages. They arose out of the need for some such machinery for discussion and negotiation; but they are equally, and increasingly, concerned with the prevention of disputes and with reaching settlement without resort to the strike or lock-out.

35

We must now see what means are available for preventing and settling disputes.

Subjects for inquiry and discussion

1. Make inquiries into the history of the Trade Union movement in your locality.
2. What is the present function of a Friendly Society? Find out which of the Societies were most prominent in your locality fifty years ago.
3. Why were the Taff Vale (1901) and Osborne (1909) judgments of such importance?
4. Study Diagram IX. Can you explain the big drop in membership about 1930?
5. Make a list of the six largest Unions in the country.
6. Study the organisation of one Trade Union in your locality.
7. Discuss the pros and cons of restrictive practices. Find out if any are in force locally.
8. Invite (*a*) a Branch Secretary and (*b*) a Shop Steward to talk to you or your group about their Trade Union work.
9. Discuss the policy of the 'closed shop'.
10. To what Unions would the following belong: plumber, lorry driver, gas-fitter, bricklayer, merchant seaman, carpenter, dustman, railway porter, engine driver, farm worker, house painter, shop assistant?
11. Study a copy of the report of the last Trades Union Congress.
12. Why has there been so much argument about whether members should contract-in or contract-out for subscribing to Union political funds? Should Unions have political funds?
13. It is sometimes said that the Unions are not interested in the standard of work done by their members. How much truth is there in this statement?
14. What is the difference between a strike and a lock-out? When do you consider either to be justified?

CHAPTER 4

EMPLOYERS AND EMPLOYED

DURING 1919, two years after the First World War, 2,591,000 workers were involved in strikes with a loss of 34,969,000 working days; during 1947, two years after the Second World War, 620,000 workers went on strike with the loss of 2,398,000 days. Several reasons can be put forward for this considerable difference; one of the most effective causes has been the increasing use of the ways and means available for settling disputes. Employers and workers have found that the strike or the lock-out is a wasteful method of forcing a solution to grievances; moreover, the experience of closer working and consultation during the Second World War, and the subsequent economic problems that industry has had to face, have encouraged a habit of discussion round the table.

Mention was made in Chapter 2 of some ways in which wage regulation by the State has been extended to a number of industries. Here something should be said of other ways that have been devised for the prevention, or settlement, of disputes.[1] But first it should be noted that the Ministry of Labour has very limited powers of compulsion in industrial disputes; the principle followed has always been to encourage both employers and employed to set up their own organisations for the settlement of disputes. State interference has been kept to a minimum, but recommendations are made for improving methods of settlement and some machinery has been established for the use of

[1] The *Industrial Relations Handbook* (H.M.S.O.) should be studied for further details.

those who want it. One result has been a great variety of councils, committees, and so on, established by the industries to suit individual conditions. It is not therefore possible to give in a few pages a full account of these many organisations; all we can do is to describe the main pattern.

WHITLEY COMMITTEE. In 1917 an important committee was set up by the Government under the chairmanship of J. H. Whitley (later Speaker of the House of Commons):

'(1) to make and consider suggestions for securing a permanent improvement in the relations between employers and workmen; and

'(2) to recommend means for securing that industrial conditions affecting the relations between employers and workmen shall be systematically reviewed by those concerned, with a view to improving conditions in the future.'

The recommendations made by the Whitley Committee have been the basis of many later developments. Five suggestions were made:

1. Well organized industries should have Joint Industrial Councils.
2. Each factory or business should have a Works Committee representative of both sides.
3. Badly organized trades should be subject to wage-regulation by the State. (This we have already described in Chapter 2.)
4. A permanent Court of Arbitration should be set up.
5. The Minister of Labour should have power to hold an inquiry into any dispute.

All these suggestions have been put into effect.

JOINT INDUSTRIAL COUNCILS. A Joint Industrial Council is described in the Whitley Report as 'an organization, representative of employers and workpeople, to have as its object the regular consideration of matters affecting the progress and well-being of the trade from the point of view of all those engaged in it, so far as is consistent with the general interest of the community'. The Committee gave as suitable subjects for the consideration of such Councils:

better use of the practical experience of the workers,
settlement of general conditions of employment,
technical training,
industrial research,
improvement in methods.

The Government itself established a National Whitley Council for the Civil Service, and Industrial Councils in all departments. Local Authorities have also accepted this method. It will be noted that the name 'Joint Industrial Council' is not always used; 'Conciliation Board' is a common alternative, and teachers have the 'Burnham Committee' (named after its first chairman) for dealing with salaries. But whatever the name, the object and purpose are the same, though some industries have gone further than others in covering the list of subjects set out above. A great number of the Councils now exist, ranging from the National Joint Council for the Building Industry to the Gelatine and Glue Joint Industrial Council.

WORKS COMMITTEES. The second recommendation of the Whitley Committee has also seen results in the setting up of Works Committees. These may be regarded as more local bodies than the Joint Councils. Their purpose according to the Whitley Committee is:

' (1) to give employees wider interest in and greater responsibility for the conditions in which their work is performed;

(2) to enforce the regulations in collective agreements drawn up by the District and National Authorities; and (3) to prevent friction and misunderstanding.'

During and since the Second World War two other means have been used for increasing co-operation between employers and employed. Joint Production Committees and Management Advisory Committees have been set up in a number of industries to discuss how to avoid waste of labour and of materials, and how to increase efficiency and output. The second method was the formation of what were called Working Parties; these consisted of representative employers and workers together with independent members; their job was to study the position and prospects of the industries concerned. This method was not intended to become a permanent part of industrial consultation, but as the results were encouraging the the same method may well be used again.[1]

It should be noted that there is no one rigid pattern of collaboration laid down that all must follow; each industry adapts the general idea or scheme to suit its own conditions. All such meetings of employers and employed as are concerned with general matters as distinct from wage regulation are helping to break down the traditional suspicions between both parties. The pace may be slow, and sometimes there are halts and even breakdowns, but we are still in the early stages of this new road for industrial development.

STRIKES. In spite of all these preventative methods, strikes do occur. Sometimes we feel that the reasons given for such stoppages are trivial and we are apt to jump to

[1]The reports of these Working Parties, published for the Board of Trade by H.M.S.O., contain much valuable information on such industries as furniture, boots and shoes, pottery, etc. The earliest was published in 1946.

unwise conclusions. Before passing judgment on any strike we should make every effort to find out the underlying causes; this is admittedly difficult, but it is important to do so. The grievances today are of a different character from those typical of the 1920s. The strikers may have lost patience with the slow working of the negotiating machinery and feel that it needs speeding up; or they may believe that their Unions are not pressing their claims strongly enough; or they may resent the treatment of one or more of their fellows. Part of the difficulty lies, as has already been mentioned, in the vast size of some of the Unions—such, for instance, as the Transport and General Workers Union. Such Unions contain men doing a wide variety of jobs, and one group may feel that its interests are being overlooked. There is, too, the loss of personal touch between the 'bosses' at the top and the men in the workshop. The men may therefore start an 'unofficial strike'—that is, one not called by the Union executive committee. This is one of the problems the Unions must solve themselves.

We must now consider the means available for settling disputes where the parties concerned are unable to reach agreement through the various Councils and other bodies so far described.

ARBITRATION. The services of the Ministry of Labour are available as an aid in settling disputes. There is an Industrial Relations Department at the Ministry which is prepared to act as mediator or arbitrator or to give any other kind of useful help if the parties in the dispute are willing to use its services. That last clause is important; it sums up the policy of the industrial legislation of this century as far as disputes are concerned—that is, the parties are encouraged to settle the matter themselves;

only when that fails is the Ministry prepared to help by way of advice or arbitration.

The Minister of Labour can act in the following ways:

(1) When the parties in a dispute are unable to reach agreement, he can, at the request of either or both, appoint a conciliator, or a board of conciliation, to help in finding a solution. The Ministry's Conciliation Officers are available at all times, and many disputes have been settled by their aid. The extent of this work is not generally realised as it does not provide news for the papers; a strike has much more news value.

(2) The Industrial Courts Act of 1919 set up (in accordance with the suggestions of the Whitley Committee) a permanent National Arbitration Tribunal to arbitrate in disputes if both parties so wish. Later Acts, such as the Road Traffic Act of 1930, have given more importance to this Tribunal, and some industries (especially those that have been nationalised) have special Tribunals for considering wage and other claims.

(3) The Minister can also appoint a single arbitrator (with assessors) where this method is helpful.

(4) The Act of 1919 also empowered the Minister to appoint special Boards of Arbitration (or *ad hoc* Boards) to deal with particular disputes. Such a Board usually consists of an independent chairman and one representative of each party in the dispute.

(5) The Minister can also institute a Court of Enquiry where the serious character of the dispute, or its prolonged nature, shows the need for an impartial study of facts and causes. Such a Court can be set up without the consent of the disputants; it can require the production of information and documents and take evidence on oath. Its findings cannot be enforced, but are laid

before Parliament, which can, if it so decides, legislate. The publicity of such an Enquiry is usually sufficient to mend affairs.

(6) The Minister can also appoint a Committee of Investigation to inquire into the causes of a dispute. This is a less formidable affair than a Court of Enquiry, and the findings are not laid before Parliament.

From all this it can be seen that there is in existence a number of methods for dealing with industrial disputes. As was pointed out at the beginning of this chapter, these ways and means of conciliation, arbitration and inquiry have gradually helped to decrease the number of disputes that have resulted in strikes. The right to strike remains as the last weapon in the hands of the workers but its use will probably be called for more rarely in the future. Such strikes as do occur will probably be, in the main, outbreaks of impatience in sections of an industry rather than throughout a whole industry.

The means of settlement exist if the disputants seriously wish to avoid open rupture.

The Government has powers in reserve for taking direct action when a strike threatens essential supplies and services. Under the Emergency Powers Act of 1939 it can declare a state of emergency and take the necessary steps to maintain essential supplies. This was done during a Dock Strike in July, 1949; but the dockers returned to work when a state of emergency was declared. These special powers were continued after the Second World War in view of the subsequent economic difficulties. In this restricted sense a strike can be declared to be illegal.

Subjects for inquiry and discussion

1. Do you think there should be a system of compulsory arbitration in industrial disputes ? How would such a system work ?

2. Study the system of arbitration established in Australia.

3. What industries in your locality have (*a*) Joint Industrial Councils, and (*b*) Works Committees ? Discuss, with people employed in these firms, their constitutions and how they work.

4. Should the Working Party become a permanent part of our industrial organization ? How would it differ in membership and functions from a Joint Industrial Council ?

5. What is the procedure to be followed when railway porters claim an increase in wages ? What considerations would have to be taken into account in making a decision ?

6. Make a careful study of a recent strike. What were the declared reasons ? Were there deeper causes ? What part did the Ministry of Labour play in it ? Was it worth it ?

7. Read up the history of (*a*) the Dock Strike of 1889 and (*b*) the Dockers' Inquiry of 1920. Compare the methods used in reaching a settlement.

8. Why is a Court of Enquiry seldom set up ? Study the report of a recent Court. Would it be a good thing to have such an Enquiry in every dispute ?

9. It has been suggested that all strikes should be made illegal. How could such a law be enforced ?

10. Can you suggest any additional ways in which industrial disputes could be settled without strike action ?

CHAPTER 5

THE ORGANISATION OF INDUSTRY

So FAR we have been considering the national economy from the point of view of the salary or wage earner who is primarily interested in making a living. We must now see how industry is organised.

A reference to Diagram VI (p. 16) will show what a large part of the population is engaged in producing things. Here are some of the leading industries, arranged in descending order of the number they employ.

> Engineering
> Building
> Metal goods (such as stoves, electrical apparatus, tools, etc.)
> Textiles (such as cotton, woollens, hosiery, carpets, etc.)
> Coal-mining
> Motor manufacture
> Agriculture
> Clothing
> Paper, printing, etc.
> Iron and steel
> Chemicals, paints, etc.

MASS-PRODUCTION. One of the characteristics of British industry is the variety in the size and methods of organisation of firms. We get so accustomed to seeing the names of the very big firms that we forget the large number of small manufacturers who contribute an appreciable

45

proportion of the whole output. Thus a town may have a great steel works as its main industry, yet nearby may be the workshop of an independent producer employing half a dozen men in the making of one article, such as knives. Some things, such as tractors, can best be produced by mass-methods, that is, by making use of standardised machine-processes that can be carried out by semi-skilled machine-minders instead of by skilled men. Varieties of types and of parts are reduced to a minimum, so that the final product is put together on what is called the 'assembly line' in an automatic manner calling for dexterity rather than for specialised skill. The 'conveyor belt' (first used systematically by Henry Ford in 1912) may be regarded as the symbol of this kind of production. By this method costs are reduced by making it possible to make large numbers of one article. The whole process is the result of carrying two ideas as far as possible:

(1) *division of labour,* whereby the parts of a task are divided so that each worker has a small job to do and does not spend time passing from job to job or from tool to tool;

(2) *standardisation,* whereby operations are made as uniform as practicable and reduced to a routine.

It is wrong, however, to think of British industry as being mainly, or even largely, of the mass-production type. Our long tradition of individual skill and craftsmanship is too valuable even from a commercial point of view for it to be pushed on one side. The struggle for markets that has been going on for some years has proved that there is a leading part to be played by products that have the finish and perfection that only individual skill can give.

The general picture, therefore, of our industry is of a wide variety of forms: some firms produce on a large scale; others are small and produce highly finished goods.

The big factory calls for elaborate organisation with a number of departments each under a manager. Thus under the managing director there may be an accountant and secretary, a works manager, a sales manager, and perhaps an advertising or publicity manager, a chief designer, and a welfare or personnel officer. Each of these will have his subordinate officers and staff organised in a hierarchy of duties and responsibilities. On the workers' side will be the shop steward and the representatives on the Works Committee. Management has indeed become a profession of its own, calling for special abilities, training and experience.

All this is a far cry from the small workshop where the employer does all the managing and probably shares in the actual work. From the human point of view it may be felt that the small, independent workshop is preferable, since the individual does not lose his identity and become an automaton endlessly repeating the same motions at the assembly line. Our national economy needs both forms of industry and the tradition of good design and construction can be preserved even in mass-production. Nor should it be forgotten that some workers prefer a mechanical task to one in which they have to exercise personal judgment.

CAPITAL. Whatever the size of an industry, there will be need for capital when it begins and for later expansion. The word 'capital' is frequently misunderstood and misused, so it calls for an explanation. The term 'capitalist' is indeed sometimes used as a reproach, especially when it is coupled with the adjective 'bloated'. For our purpose we must forget such tendentious uses and consider the

subject of capital with as much detachment as we have
discussed the subject of population.

In Dr. Johnson's Dictionary (1785) the word 'capital'
is not given in the sense used here. He defines 'capital
stock' as 'the principal or original stock of a trader, or
company.' It will help us to get our own ideas clear if we
remember this earlier use of the term.

Whatever business enterprise a man undertakes, he will
need something to start with, even if it is only a spade and
fork to begin digging a small-holding. Anyone who wants
to open a shop needs premises and a stock of goods, and
something to live on while he is building up his connexion
of customers. He may, of course, borrow the money with
which to pay for all this, but the lender will need some
security on the loan as well as the payment of interest.
It is wrong to think of the capital as simply the money
value of what is needed; that is a convenient way of
expressing the total outlay; it is better to think of capital
as the land, premises, equipment, raw materials, and so
on, that are needed.

Many of our biggest industrial firms began as one-man
or family affairs, or as a partnership between two or three
men, each of whom provided part of the initial capital and
afterwards shared in the profits on an agreed scale. Such
a small business could remain small if the owner or
owners were content and used the profits for their personal
purposes. But few are content with remaining as they
are ; they wish to make progress (measured in profits and
extent of business). Some of the profits must then be
saved and used as new capital to build a bigger factory,
or buy another shop. So capital also represents savings
which have been deliberately put on one side in order to
expand a business. The original capital also represented

savings either by the founder or, if he borrowed money, by other people.

SHAREHOLDERS. The time may come in the progress of a business when the possibilities of expansion are so good that the original owners cannot save the additional capital required, so they invite others to take shares in the business, that is, to become shareholders. Each shareholder is entitled to a part of the profits (if any) in proportion to the amount of money he has invested in the business.

Some industries cannot begin on a small capital because the initial costs of equipment, new buildings, and so on are too great. For instance it has been estimated that to start a national daily newspaper before 1939 needed a capital of perhaps two million pounds. It is difficult, for example, to believe that a new motor factory could to-day be built up on the work of one man beginning as Lord Nuffield did by repairing bicycles and then gradually changing over to making motor cycles and so to the first Morris Oxford car. Some new form of manufacture may offer similar opportunities and a man of initiative may take the chance to found a business. Generally speaking, to-day new industrial businesses cannot be established without considerable capital. It is for this reason that the Government now gives assistance in the building and equipment of factories, power stations, and so on, that will help industrial development.

When a new business is proposed, or the expansion of an established one is desired, an invitation is issued to the public to take shares. Naturally those who consider the project want to have full particulars of the scheme so that they can be satisfied that it has a reasonable chance of success. There are rogues who gull people by false promises of the get-rich-quickly kind, but the law deals severely with them when they are caught. There are strict regulations by law about the issue of proposals for forming companies—that is, Joint Stock Companies consisting of shareholders who provide the capital. The prospectus for such a company must give all relevant information, the names of the promoters, and so on. Moreover, after the company has been established it must issue balance sheets and reports giving a true account of the position each year.

'Co., Ltd.' The term 'Company, Limited' we see so frequently (or 'Co., Ltd.'—in U.S.A., 'Inc.', meaning 'incorporated') indicates that the business is capitalised in this manner. The 'Limited' shows that each shareholder's liability is limited to the amount of money he invests. So if the company goes bankrupt, each investor is responsible only for his share of the capital and not for all the obligations of the company.

There are several kinds of shares.

1. *Ordinary shares.*

The holders of these shares nominally control the company; they appoint directors to look after the business management, and they can, if they so wish, change the directors at an annual meeting. A report is then presented to the shareholders on the state of the business. Actually few shareholders bother to take any active part in the annual meeting, and it is only when there is a threat of loss or serious difficulty that they attend in large numbers. The interest (or dividend) received by the shareholder depends on the amount of profit (if any) made during each year; it therefore varies according to the prosperity of the company.

It should be noted that not all the profit is divided amongst the shareholders; some is put on one side (undistributed) to pay for replacements of machinery, etc., or for improving the business. This process of using part of the profits for further development is sometimes called 'ploughing back' into the business some of its proceeds.

2. *Preference shares.*

These shares carry a fixed rate of interest which does not change according to the fortunes of the company and the holders are given preference as to payment before other shareholders. Since holders of such shares run less risk than ordinary shareholders they have less voting power in the annual meetings.

Each of these two main kinds of shares has several varieties, the differences being marked by methods of payment of dividends and by powers of control in the company affairs.

3. *Debentures.*

Strictly speaking, these are not shares; they are loans on which interest has to be paid until the principal is repaid. The buyers of debentures are creditors of the company concerned. The holders are represented by trustees who watch their interests but have no say in the management of affairs.

The shareholders are not always individual investors. Banks, insurance and building societies, and other bodies are large shareholders in all kinds of industrial enterprises. These use the savings of individuals deposited with them for commercial investment. A private person who has saved some money often prefers to put it into one of these big concerns under expert control rather than risk making a direct investment on his own judgment. He gets a lower rate of interest than he might if he were a direct share-holder, but his risks are reduced to a minimum. One fact should be noted: the number of individuals who have direct or indirect investments in industry is very large; or, if we choose to call them capitalists, it might be said that a fair proportion of the population can be so described. One figure will serve to illustrate this point. In 1947 the building societies of Great Britain held investments to the value of nearly 180 million pounds. Over three million persons were shareholders or depositors in these societies.

From what has been said it will be seen that many, probably most, shareholders have little or no direct concern with the businesses in which their money is invested. Just as the increase of mass-production methods has resulted in some loss of personal satisfaction in completing a good piece of work, so the impersonality of widely spread investment has meant a loss of personal concern with the welfare of an industry; the investor knows none of the workers who help to produce his dividends; he probably never sees them in the factory and has no idea of the conditions under which they work. In other words he feels no responsibility for the human conditions under which part of his income is produced. There is no simple solution for this situation; it is part of the price that has to be paid for large-scale production to meet the needs of our vast population.

THE STOCK EXCHANGE. Shares have become as much an article of commerce as refrigerators or carpets. The market where these transactions are carried out is the Stock Exchange, though the small investor will probably go to his bank. The difference between stocks and shares should be noted. A share is a fixed unit, say of £1 or £50, and the investor buys so many shares. Thus a company might have a capital of £50,000 divided into 50,000 shares of £1 each, and Mr. Brown may decide to buy

100 shares. Stock, however, can be bought in any amount that is on the market. Mr. Brown, for instance, buys £1,126 of a certain stock. The value of stocks and shares fluctuates with the prosperity of the business; thus the original £1 of a flourishing company may now be worth £5 if offered for sale because the rate of interest (on the original £1) is so high. Whatever the new price may be, the share remains a £1 share.

The Stock Exchange (the equivalent in the U.S.A. is popularly called 'Wall Street') is conducted under strict rules and safeguards, but there are some speculators who gamble on a rise or fall in the value of stocks and shares; they serve no useful function in the community, but the work of the Stock Exchange itself has importance as it is one of the ways by which capital flows into industry.

COPARTNERSHIP. One form of industrial organisation calls for a brief notice as it is based on an attractive idea. Under copartnership and profit-sharing schemes the workers themselves may own some of the capital and benefit directly in the prosperity of their firms. There are a number of variations of the main idea; each firm that adopts it frames its own system. One scheme is that a bonus is paid in the form of a share or part of a share, when profits rise above an agreed figure; thus the more prosperous the firm, the more shares are held by the workers themselves. Attractive as this idea is on paper, comparatively few such schemes have been put into effect for any long period. In 1938 there were only 256 such undertakings (outside the Co-operative Societies) affecting at most 200,000 workers, or less than one per cent of the working population.

CARTELS AND TRUSTS. In the previous chapter something was said of associations of employers for the purpose

of negotiating with the workers. Another form of association calls for mention. Trusts and cartels are associations
of industrial firms engaged in the same kind of production
for the purpose of promoting and protecting their trade
interests. A cartel (a term more frequently used for international associations) is concerned with controlling production so that too many goods may not be put on the
market at once and thus bring down the price. Each firm
in a cartel retains control of its own management. Such
cartels are generally concerned with basic materials or
manufactures in an early stage, such as steel, cables,
potash, etc. A trust is an organisation to control under one
central authority a group of firms; that is, each business is
not allowed full freedom in its own working but must con-
form to the scheme laid down by the central board. The
trust may try to buy up, or squeeze out, any rivals and
thus may create a monopoly; this means that a few men
are in a position to control production and prices to the
detriment of the public.

The danger of this kind of trust has not been felt
acutely in this country because contracts leading to a
restraint of trade against the public interest are not
enforceable at law. Moreover there is a strong public
opinion against monopolies—this is of old standing, for
it found expression as far back as the days of Queen
Elizabeth. In the U.S.A. several attempts have been made
to control trusts by law.

Subjects for inquiry and discussion

1. Make a list of industries in your locality. Group them
   according to the number of men employed in each : e.g.
   under 10, 11 to 20, etc.

54

2. Do any industries in your locality make use of the assembly line or conveyor belt system? If so, get permission to watch the working.

3. What kinds of articles are suited to mass-production?

4. Compare mass-produced articles, e.g. in a Woolworth's Store, with similar articles produced by individual methods. Note particularly standard of workmanship and price.

5. Visit a large industrial works and ask permission to see the organisation chart. Study its arrangement of duties and responsibilities.

6. What do you consider to be the desirable qualifications of (a) a general manager (or managing director) and (b) a welfare (or personnel) officer?

7. What human qualities are wasted or lost in mass-production? Can you suggest how these, or some of them, could be saved?

8. Give instances (local if possible) of large businesses that have developed out of one-man efforts.

9. Watch in the newspapers or weekly journals for an announcement of a new issue of shares in a company. Get a copy of the prospectus and study it carefully, assuming that you have £500 to invest. What points would you consider in making your decision?

10. Watch the newspapers also for any reports of cases tried in the courts of fraudulent offers of shares.

11. Study the annual report and balance sheet of a local or national company.

12. Can you suggest ways in which shareholders could be encouraged to take a greater interest in the welfare of those employed in the industries in which they have invested?

13. Find out what the following terms mean on the Stock Exchange: broker, jobber, bulls, bears.

14. Why is it that copartnership and profit-sharing schemes have rarely proved attractive? Are there any firms in

your locality where such schemes are established ? If so, talk the matter over with one of the workers.

15. Read up the story of one of the big United States Trusts, e.g. the Standard Oil Company, or the Steel Corporation. (The biographies of John D. Rockefeller and Andrew Carnegie would supply what you want.) Has anything comparable been built up in this country, e.g. in cocoa, soap, and sugar ?

CHAPTER 6

THE STATE IN INDUSTRY

WE have already noted several ways in which the Government legislates for industry, such as by the enforcement of healthy conditions of working, the regulation of wages in some trades, the provision of means for conciliation, and so on. Such measures do not entail direct organisation or control of industry by the State; they lay down certain safeguards for the workers that good employers would normally provide. The purpose of the State here is to bring the bad or indifferent employers in line with others.

Up to this century the Government has kept an eye on industry, often for financial reasons, but has not assumed full direction. By means of agreements with other countries, the development of trade has been encouraged, and laws have been passed to foster the prosperity of some industries. Thus the series of Navigation Laws enacted from the fourteenth century until the nineteenth aimed at giving English shipping a monopoly of sea-borne trade to and from this country; for example, the Navigation Act of 1672 restricted trade with the Plantations or Colonies to English ships; this became one of the grievances leading to the war with the American Colonies.

Another type of legislation is illustrated by the Acts for Burying in Woollen passed in the reign of Charles II and not repealed until 1814. This was intended to encourage the woollen industry; it enacted that everyone must be buried in a shroud of 'sheep's wool'. Regulations such as the two described were gradually withdrawn during the nineteenth century in keeping with the principle that dominated the period of non-interference by the State in industry; the term *laissez-faire* is usually applied to this principle. It was invoked by the opponents—some of them good men—of legislation to regulate the labour of children in mines and factories.

THE END OF *LAISSEZ-FAIRE*. To-day we are familiar with the idea of the Government taking an active part in directing the industrial life of the country by various regulations and controls affecting supplies of raw materials, the amount of production and the disposal of the results. What has caused this change in policy? Several contributory influences may be noted.

1. Great Britain no longer enjoys the opportunities for trade she had in the nineteenth century. Many of our customers in other countries during that period now produce for themselves the things they used to buy from us, or protect their industries by tariffs. Appeals to the Government from industries suffering from loss of markets or from crippling competition have resulted in State action to stimulate trade. Indeed it has now become customary for industries when they get into difficulties to assume that it is the business of the Government to get them out of their difficulties. This is a complete revolution in attitude.

2. During the Second World War we had to sell many of our investments in foreign countries to pay for the war. These used to help us to balance our trade. This loss has proved an additional limitation of markets. More must be said on these two points in a later chapter.

58

3. There is a general desire for a better standard of living and for decreasing the gap between riches and poverty. Better wages, family allowances, National Insurance and other means have been devised to meet this desire. The cost of such benefits comes ultimately from industry, and the Government is thus forced to take steps to promote the prosperity of industry. We may think of the money as coming from taxes (i.e. from our pockets) or from contributions we make to insurance schemes (again, from our pockets), but what is in our pockets comes from earnings which depend on the success of industry. If industry fails, then we cannot meet the bill for a higher standard of living.

4. Socialist doctrines that have been propagated and widely accepted during this century necessitate Government ownership and control. The Oxford English Dictionary defines socialism as 'a theory or policy of social organization which advocates the ownership and control of the means of production, capital, land, property, etc. by the community as a whole, and their administration or distribution in the interests of all.' This is not the place to discuss, even briefly, the merits and demerits of this political doctrine; here it is only necessary to note that its translation into action inevitably means a far greater degree of governmental control than has been regarded as desirable in the past.

Had there been no Second World War, the same problems would have had to be faced at some later period; the war hastened the great change from the open markets of the last century to the restricted markets of this. We must also keep in mind the problems of supporting our great population that were noted in the first chapter. (Refer again to Diagram I and note the increase in population since 1870.) Whatever political party forms a Government, the same questions would have to be studied. The method chosen immediately after the Second World War was that of an economy planned by the Government either through controls or by national ownership.

The term 'nationalisation' has become part of our common speech; the plain meaning of the word is that the State takes over the ownership of an industry, but in its practical application nationalisation may cover various forms and degrees of control and ownership.

PUBLIC UTILITY SERVICES. There is nothing novel in the idea of the State or a local authority (such as a county or borough) owning and conducting enterprises for the benefit of the community. We are familiar, for instance, with the Post Office as a national business, and with municipal transport services. These are examples of things done for our common benefit; similarly we can regard the railways (nationalised in 1947), electricity (1947), and gas (1949). The term 'Public Utility Service' has been applied to such undertakings. They have become essentials for our kind of civilisation. Under State control it is possible to extend their benefits to parts of the country where a private firm would find it unprofitable to work. Town-dwellers going into the country for a holiday are sometimes shocked to find that the water supply is drawn from wells or even from rainwater butts; no private firm could afford to provide such places with piped water, so it is necessary for the State to accept the responsibility. So, too, remote farms cannot be supplied by private firms with electricity, since the initial cost is prohibitive, but if the whole country is treated as the unit of operation under State organisation, then the costs of extension to out-of-the-way places can be spread nationally.

Between such public service undertakings and privately owned businesses there is a great variety of what may be called mixed enterprises in which the State exercises some measure of control.

THE PUBLIC CORPORATION. A form of organisation has been developed in this country which attempts to combine the advantages of national ownership with those of private enterprise. The Public Corporation, as it is known, has been arrived at through experiment in our traditional manner. We are still learning how to make this kind of organisation more efficient; the period of trial and error is sometimes annoying, but it is unavoidable; the important thing is that we should learn from our mistakes and adapt our institutions accordingly so that they are constantly improving.

A Public Corporation is created by Act of Parliament to conduct an industrial or other undertaking in the interests of the whole community. It is not a Department of State, nor is it run from one of the Ministries ('from Whitehall', as the phrase is) but by a board appointed by the Government. Once the board has been appointed (usually for a term of years) it has full freedom of working just like any other board of directors; it is not, however, responsible to a body of shareholders, but to the Government. We have seen how shareholders, generally speaking, rarely exercise the rights they have in private companies; the Government is in a position to step in when a Public Corporation fails to fulfil its purpose. Day-to-day administration is carried out under the direction of the board through its regional representatives. The financial side of each undertaking is conducted on the lines of usual commercial practice. The accounts are not included in the national balance sheet and each undertaking is expected to pay its own way and, if possible, produce a profit that can be applied to reducing the cost to the consumer.

B.B.C. The best known example of a Public Corporation is the British Broadcasting Corporation, established in 1927. Broadcasting could have been done, as in other countries, by private companies competing with each other and drawing their revenue from programmes sponsored by commercial firms desiring to advertise their goods. It was decided in this country to create a State monopoly, but so constituted that the actual conduct and content of the programmes should be almost completely independent of Government control. Finance was provided by a licence fee on receiving-sets—ten shillings up to 1946, and after that, one pound. Nearly twelve million licences were taken out in 1949. Parliament makes a special grant for some important services, such as overseas broadcasting. Licences are bought at post offices, and the Postmaster-General is the Minister responsible for the B.B.C. The Corporation is directed by a board of seven governors appointed by the Government; the governors appoint the director-general, who is the chief officer. All questions of programmes, staffing and so on are left to the board and the director-general. The Government does not interfere with these normal activities, but official announcements must be broadcast if required. Once a year the accounts are presented to Parliament and this gives an opportunity for debate and the making of criticisms. Questions cannot be asked in Parliament on day-to-day matters such as the content of programmes.

The B.B.C. may be taken as a type of the organisation so far adopted for nationalised industries. Broadcasting itself is as much an industry as the theatre or cinema, and it is closely linked with the radio industry. When the coal industry was nationalised in 1946 a National Coal Board was set up of eight members nominated by the Government; this board is free to organise and develop the industry on whatever lines it thinks best. The annual report provides an opportunity for discussion in Parliament, but, as with the B.B.C., questions on details of working are not allowed.

We may note two ways in which a nationalised industry differs from private business. Its primary purpose is not to produce profits for shareholders, but, by efficient working, reduce costs to consumers, while at the same time paying its way and maintaining a sound standard of wages and conditions of labour. Secondly, the need for presenting an annual report with a statement of accounts provides an opportunity for debate in Parliament, when grievances can be made public. Such open discussion is not possible in the affairs of a private undertaking.

COAL. The nationalisation of the coal industry marked a new stage in State control of industry. Such undertakings as railways, electricity and gas can be regarded as public services; but, however important coal is to industry and home comfort, it is not on quite the same footing as a service. The stormy history of the coal mines seemed to many to justify nationalisation as the only way out of the impasse. But when it was proposed and eventually decided to nationalise the iron and steel industries, much stronger opposition was roused. This was a direct taking-over by the State of a flourishing industry. The case for and against cannot be argued here, and experience of the working of the Iron and Steel Corporation will be needed before a judgment can be made of this application of the idea of nationalisation. One of the problems is to know where to draw the line between an essential industry that is in the nature of a public service and industries that hitherto have been conducted by private enterprise. That is one of the questions we shall all have to think over.

It is possible to note some problems that have already risen in the coal industry, the utility services, and even the B.B.C. These can best be included in the subjoined list of subjects for discussion.

Subjects for inquiry and discussion

1. Study the working of the Navigation Laws. Would it be a wise policy to revive this form of legislation in aid of our shipping?
2. Early in this century the straw-hat, or 'boater', was commonly worn by men in the summer months (see *Punch.*) Then it suddenly went out of use, and the straw-hat industry was affected. What action, if any, could the Government have taken to help this industry?
3. One sometimes hears people say that 'the Government' will pay for this or that benefit. How would you convince such people that the money ultimately comes from industry?
4. Summarise the arguments for and against the socialist doctrine set out in the definition quoted above from the Oxford English Dictionary.
5. Ask half a dozen friends what they understand by the term 'nationalisation'.
6. Make a list of Public Utility Services now under State control. Can you suggest other industries that might come under this category?
7. Find out in a rural area if the farms and villages have a main electricity supply. Where does their drinking water come from?
8. Do you think it would be better to allow broadcasting to be done in this country by commercial companies in

competition, as in the U.S.A.? State the reasons for and against our present system.

9. Study the history of the coal industry in this country during this century. Was nationalisation inevitable?

10. The appointment by the Government of the members of the boards of nationalised industries is open to the danger of political favouritism—that is, appointing members because they support the party in power ('jobs for the boys'), and not for their knowledge of the industry. Are there any signs of this being done? How can this be avoided?

11. It is said that under nationalisation the workers are too remote from the national board to have any personal interest in the central control. Can you suggest ways in which this relationship could be strengthened?

12. It is argued that if the workers had a larger share in the management of a nationalised industry they would be more anxious than they are to make it efficient and prosperous. How could this be done?

13. A nationalised industry, it is said, cannot supply the same incentives to good work as a private concern. Examine the kinds of incentives to be found in private industry and consider how these, or some alternatives, could be introduced in a nationalised industry.

14. Study the last report available of one of the nationalised industries.

15. How much truth is there in the criticisms that a nationalised industry (a) is more expensive in administration, and (b) tends to send prices up?

16. If a customer does not like the goods he buys from a private firm or shop he complains to the manager or shopkeeper, or he goes elsewhere. It is a more complicated and tedious business to complain to a nationalised industry, and there is no alternative source of supply. How can the consumers' rights be safeguarded in a nationalised industry?

CHAPTER 7

DISTRIBUTION

IN the previous chapters we have been considering labour and production; we must now turn our attention to the ways in which the results of production come to us, that is, how they are distributed. It will be useful first of all to see how we spend our earnings. The following list of 1949 states money values in millions of pounds.

Food	..	..	..	..	£2,381
Alcoholic Drink	..	..	..	..	719
Tobacco	..	..	..	..	764
Rent, Rates and Water Charges	..	..	613
Fuel and Light	.... ..	..	..	349
Durable Household Goods	..	..	481
Other Household Goods	..	..	..	94
Clothing	..	..	..	..	948
Books, Newspapers and Magazines	..	136
Private Motoring	..	..	..	..	102
Travel	..	..	..	..	341
Post Office (Communication Services)	..	59
Entertainments	..	..	..	..	174
Other	..	..	..	..	1,241

TOTAL .. £8,402

The largest item in the above list is food, so it will be as well if this is broken up into its constituents. The figures that follow give the consumption in pounds weight per head, first for an average pre-war year, and secondly for 1949.

Annual consumption in lb. per head	Pre-war	1949
Dairy products (milk solids) ..	38.3 lbs.	52.6 lbs.
Meat (edible weight)	109.6	74.5
Fish, game, poultry, etc. (edible weight)	32·8	35·5

66

Eggs and egg products (shell egg equivalent)	24.0	22.7
Oils and fats (fat content)	45.3	44.0
Sugar and syrups (sugar content)	109.9	91.0
Potatoes	176.0	251.0
Pulses and nuts	9.6	8.8
Tomatoes and fruit (fresh equivalent) ..	141.5	134.4
Vegetables	107.4	107.1
Grain products	210.1	240.0
Tea, coffee and cocoa	14.7	13.9

The 1949 list is, of course, affected by rationing.

Diagram X (p. 68) shows the proportions of the main foods that we produce ourselves in comparison with what we are obliged to import.

RETAIL TRADE. We buy most of these things from retail shops; the verb 'to retail' means to sell in small quantities. The retailer buys his supplies from a wholesale merchant, who buys in large quantities from the producer. Thus the farmer sells his potatoes by the ton to the wholesale potato dealer, who, in turn, distributes them to the greengrocer (the retailer), who sells them to the housewife by the pound. Sometimes the producer and the housewife grumble at the difference between the price paid to the first and that paid by the second; he feels that he does not get enough and she that the price is too high. Between them are two middlemen, the wholesaler and the retailer, each of whom, as well as the producer, must make a profit on his transaction if he is to make a living. The dispute is usually about the amount of profit the middlemen expect. It must, however, be remembered that they have to consider a number of costs in deciding prices—such as transport, labour, rent, advertisements, etc. As we shall see presently, some big firms of retailers are able to cut out the wholesaler by buying direct from the producer, and some are their own producers. This is one way in which prices can be lowered.

EARNING AND SPENDING

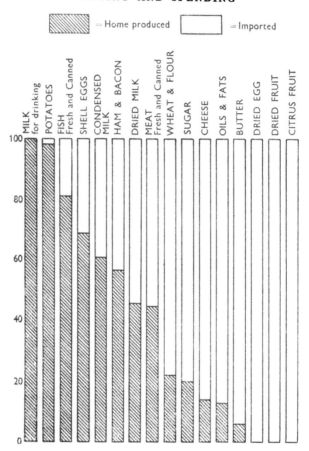

Diagram X—Main Foods, 1949

68

There are three main types of retail trade:

1. The market.
2. Independent shops.
3. Stores, of which, for convenience of description, we can recognise five kinds, though these are not mutually exclusive; each, however, has some distinctive characteristic that affects its organisation and management:

      (i) multiple stores or shops,
     (ii) chain stores,
    (iii) departmental stores,
    (iv) help-yourself stores,
     (v) co-operatives.

1. THE MARKET. We are not here concerned with the big wholesale markets like Covent Garden and Smithfield, but with open-stall markets to be found in country towns and some large towns. Some of these markets are held in covered halls; others are in open market-places or in streets. They are controlled by the local authorities, who charge a rent and lay down rules for regulating their conduct. All kinds of goods are displayed. Farm and market-garden produce usually comes from the neighbouring countryside, and housewives welcome the chance to get their vegetables fresh from the grower. Other goods may be brought in by traders (they may be pedlars) who have a circuit of towns with different market days. They go from one to the other with their cases of clothing or household goods or whatever they sell. It is a curious life and, although overhead charges are cut to a minimum, somewhat hazardous.

These open markets have a long history behind them, and the right to have them may go back to the Middle Ages. Local authorities are sometimes tempted to get rid of them or to move them to less congested parts of the towns, but any such suggestion soon rouses opposition to interference with long-established privileges.

The amount of business done in such markets is not great in comparison with the total retail trade of the country, but they represent the earliest form of such trade.

2. INDEPENDENT SHOPS. Market stalls are run, usually, by independent traders, but it is simpler to regard them as a separate type, especially since some of them are what may be called part-time retailers; after market day they may return to their small-holdings or their workshops. In this section we shall consider independent shops.

Although they far outnumber other kinds of shops (our third group), these independent shops probably account for less than half the retail trade of the country. The business of such a shop is limited to its neighbourhood; if it is dealing in foodstuffs, it usually makes delivery of goods. These shops often create a close relationship with their customers and can give consideration to personal preferences; there is a more human contact than is possible with the large stores.

3. STORES. The use of the word 'store' for 'shop' has come back to us from the United States; the explanation is that the art or craft of retail salesmanship has been highly developed in that country and some of the methods used have been adopted over here.

(i) *Multiple stores*. Multiple shops or stores are branches of one firm, e.g. Lipton's, specialising in one group of commodities, such as groceries.

(ii) *Chain stores*. These, like multiples, are owned by one firm but have a wider choice of goods and usually keep within agreed price limits. Before the Second World War, for instance, Woolworth's fixed the price at sixpence.

but since the war it has not been possible to keep to this low figure. F. W. Woolworth started his first store in the United States in 1879 and sold articles at five and ten cents—hence the American term 'Five and Ten store'. Both multiple and chain stores have the advantage over the independent trader of buying in bulk from the manufacturer; this cuts out the need for a wholesaler and so reduces costs and consequently prices.

(iii) *Department stores*. This kind of store is really a series of shops in one building belonging to one firm. Harrod's and Selfridge's in London are familiar examples. Such a store is an attractive shopping centre and the customer who goes to buy one article may easily be lured into buying other things as he wanders through the departments.

(iv) *Help-yourself stores*. We are familiar in this country with the 'Help Yourself' Teashop; the same principle has been applied in the United States to general shopping and is being put into practice here. Alternative names used are 'Combination Store', or 'Super-market'. The customer goes round the store with a container and puts into it goods chosen off the shelves and counters; at the end of the tour he or she shows the container to a clerk, who makes out the bill. This method does away with the need for a number of counter-assistants; time is saved, and the customer has a feeling of greater freedom of selection.

(v) *Co-operatives*. We are all familiar with the 'Co-op.' It shares some of the characteristics of the multiple, chain, and department stores. Its distinctive feature is that the customers are the shareholders; they own their Co-operative Society. The word 'co-operation' simply means working together with others, but it has also acquired this particular meaning of combination for economic purposes.

The modern Co-operative movement began in 1844, when twenty-eight workers of Rochdale (Lancashire) contributed £1 each to rent and stock a small shop as the Rochdale Equitable Pioneers Society. Gradually others joined the scheme. Each member received a dividend (the 'Divi') based on the amount of his purchases. From this successful experiment has developed the co-operative movement.

It is important to remember that each Co-operative Society is a separate and independent business. Barchester Co-operative Society is independent of the Cranford Co-operative Society. Each may have branch shops in neighbouring towns. The various Societies come together for certain purposes, but this is out of good-will and not of necessity.

Anyone can become a member on paying an instalment towards a first share of £1. By law no one may own more than £200 of shares in a Co-op; the average holding is about £20. A share number is given to the new member and whatever he or she buys, nearly always for cash down, is credited to that number. Periodically a dividend is paid on the total purchases made by the member. This can be paid in cash or reinvested in the Society. The profits are used partly to extend business (as capital), partly for social and educational purposes, and partly to pay the dividend.

The affairs of each Society are controlled by a committee of management elected by the members, each having one vote irrespective of his holding in shares. This committee carries out the functions of the board of directors of a company. The manager and staff are employed in the same manner as in any other business.

So far we have been considering the co-operatives as retailers, but early in their history they found that it was not always easy to get the supplies they wanted from the usual wholesalers; there was (and, indeed, there still is) a prejudice against the co-operatives because they worked on unfamiliar principles that seemed to threaten the private trader. So the Societies got together in the sixties of last century and began building up their own wholesale business. The Co-operative Wholesale Society, Ltd.(C.W.S.) is a federation for wholesale business of the retail Societies of England and Wales. There is a separate one for Scotland. The retail Societies are not obliged to get their supplies from the C.W.S., but there is every inducement to do so. All trade surplus made by the Wholesale Societies is returned to the retail Societies as dividends on purchases just as with the individual member.

The Wholesale Societies have their own factories, farms, ships, tea plantations, and so on. There is also a flourishing banking and insurance business.

Figures for 1947 will show the extent of the co-operatives.

Retail Societies	1,118
Members	9,805,300
Retail sales	£434,200,000
Wholesale sales	£275,900,000

In this country we naturally think first of the co-operative movement when the word 'Co-operative' is used. As we have seen, it was in its origin a consumers' organisation for providing, as economically as possible, the goods they needed, but we should also take note of the existence of Producers' Co-operatives. The Co-operative Productive Federation, founded in 1882, is formed of some forty productive societies with about ten thousand employees mostly engaged in the footwear and clothing trades. Some of these are controlled by the working members who are shareholders; others are run by the Consumers' Co-operatives.

Another, and very important, form of co-operative enterprise is concerned with agriculture. This developed first on the continent, and it was not until the agricultural depression in this country between the wars that it made much progress amongst us. There are two kinds of work done; the first is to supply feeding stuffs, seeds, fertilisers, etc., and the second is to market the produce, such as grain, fruit, eggs, and so on. The Agricultural Co-operative Association set up in 1945 provides a central authority; this works closely with the National Farmers' Union. There is also an Agricultural Co-operative Managers' Association. The individual societies are based on counties, e.g. the Wiltshire Farmers, or on regions, e.g. the Southern Counties Agricultural Trading Society. In addition to organising supply and sale, these societies provide expert advice.

It is interesting to note that there is close working between these societies and the older co-operative movement; thus they have a large trade with the C.W.S., who gave financial help to some in their struggling days. They have even joined together (co-operators co-operating) in such an establishment as the Herts. and Beds. Co-operative Bacon Factory.

All these forms of co-operation, both old and new, are voluntary in membership and self-governing in organisation; they are vigorous and full of promise for the future.

Figures are not available for all the types of shops described in this chapter, but the following statistics (1947) for grocers, provision merchants and general food shops are an indication of the relative proportions.

Independent retailers	120,400
Branches of multiples (i.e. with 10 or more branch shops)	15,300
Branch shops of co-operatives	10,300

74

Subjects for inquiry and discussion

1. Rearrange the items in the list on p. 66 in the order of values beginning with the highest. (Omit the item labelled 'Other'.) Make any comments that occur to you in studying your list.

2. Find out the price the producer gets for one of the common foods we eat, e.g. potatoes or eggs, and compare this with the retail price. How do you account for the difference? Can you suggest a better system that would avoid the wholesale costs and so bring down the price?

3. Study the Milk Marketing scheme in this country. How does it work? Who derives benefit from it? Why has this system not been more widely extended to other commodities?

4. Do you think it is wasteful for several bakers and milkmen to make deliveries in the same street? How would you suggest this could be avoided?

5. Spend an hour or so in an open market. Note what things are on sale. Make a list of those that are produced locally. Are the prices different from shop prices?

6. What advantages has an independent shop over one belonging to a multiple firm?

7. If you wanted to set up a stall in an open market, how would you go about it, and what regulations would you have to observe?

8. Suppose you wanted to open a shop (make your own choice of the goods to be sold) in your locality, what considerations would you have to bear in mind in making your plans? Assume that you can start anywhere.

9. Make a list of the shops in your chief shopping street. Classify them according to the list of types given in this chapter.

10. Why do chain stores, and some multiple stores, have the same design for their shop fronts wherever they are?

75

11. The idea of the chain store has come to us from the United States and has proved successful. The co-operative system has made little headway in the United States. Can you suggest any explanation of these two facts?

12. Study the history of the nearest Co-operative Society. Find out all you can about its present organisation and trade.

13. Some retailers object to the co-operatives. Find out their reasons and the answers to their objections.

14. What are the differences between a Co-operative Society and a Company owning multiple stores?

15. If you are within reach of a farming district, find out if there is any Farmers' Co-operative, or similar organisation and study its scope and organisation.

CHAPTER 8

MONEY

We receive our earnings in cash (notes or coin) or by cheque. When we buy anything we have to pay money for it. From this we may get the impression that money itself has a value; it has, it is true, a very small value in itself—that of the metal in the coins or the paper used for bank-notes. We must try to understand what money is and how it is used.

In a primitive community, or even amongst school-boys, things are bartered, or 'swopped'. But the time soon comes when this method of getting things we want becomes too complicated. Suppose a man wants a dog and has a goat to offer in exchange. The transaction is quite simple if the present owner of the dog wants a goat; but suppose he wants a pig and the owner of the goat has no pig to offer in exchange? He can of course hunt round for someone with a pig who wants a goat; then, having exchanged the goat for the pig, he can take the pig to the owner of the dog. All this assumes that dog=goat=pig. But what if 1 dog=$\frac{1}{2}$ goat=$\frac{1}{4}$ pig? It is not necessary to take the example further, as the complications of such barter soon become baffling. A solution to the difficulty was to find some commodity which could serve as a medium of exchange The early books of the Bible contain many examples of cattle, or sheep, or goats being used to measure wealth or as a medium of exchange. Such methods are still in use in parts of Africa and elsewhere.

The earliest metallic coinage of which we have any knowledge dates back to Greece in the seventh century B.C. Previously to that pieces of gold or silver were used by weight.

COINS. Precious metals are used because they are not easily obtainable and, owing to their value, can be used in small pieces that can be carried about. Lumps or bits of these metals were inconvenient because they would have to be weighed and assayed each time. So governments issued coins of a guaranteed weight and purity for use as money. Kings sometimes found it profitable to debase the coinage—that is, use metal which was not of the stated value. Our coins are made at the Mint on Tower Hill in London. Coins were minted in London before the Norman Conquest; some of King Alfred's coins were made there. Mints were also permitted in some other towns up to the reign of Edward VI. Counterfeiting coins or forging bank-notes is a most serious felony. The former crime of clipping, that is, paring metal off the edge, was made almost impossible by the introduction of the milled edge in 1663.

Gold and silver coins were originally worth the actual market value of the metal of which they were made. The earliest English coin, the silver penny, was 1/240th of a pound weight of silver. This silver penny in Norman times was known as a sterling; a pound of sterlings was 240 of these silver pennies. From this is derived the pound sterling as the unit of prices, etc., though no one has ever seen a pound sterling any more than he has seen a degree Centigrade. Another survival of the silver penny is to be found in Troy Weight, in which 240 pennyweights go to the pound Troy (which used to be called the Tower pound).

CURRENCY NOTES. During the First World War the gold sovereign (or pound) and the gold ten-shilling piece were withdrawn from use in this country; the gold, so to speak, remains in the background as a guarantee of value. Paper currency notes representing one pound and ten shillings were introduced. These were issued by the Treasury through the Bank of England (founded in 1694 as bankers to the Government, nationalised in 1946) and you will see on a note the words 'I promise to pay the Bearer on Demand the sum of One Pound [Ten Shillings]', and at the bottom the signature of the Chief Cashier of the Bank. Actually if you took a note to the Bank of England and asked for a gold sovereign, you would not get it. This is an indication of an important change that has come about; money is now regarded more as a token than as metal of so much commercial value. Our shillings and pence no longer contain the equivalent value in the metal of which they are made. The Treasury (the Government department under the Chancellor of the Exchequer) decides how much money shall be issued and the Government guarantees its validity.

BANK-NOTES AND CHEQUES. Bank-notes and cheques came into use to meet a need. In the seventeenth century (especially during the Civil Wars) people entrusted their money to goldsmiths for safe keeping. The goldsmiths gave these depositors notes saying that they could withdraw the amount deposited. Here is an example:

November 28th., 1684

I promise to pay unto the R. Honble Ye Lord North & Grey or bearer ninety pounds at demand.

for Mr. Francis Child & myself
Jno Rogers.

79

These notes themselves were found to be as good as money, as they were based on cash deposits; they were therefore used in exchange. It was not long before the cheque, as we call it, came into use. Johnson's Dictionary defines a 'check' as 'the correspondent cipher of a bank bill'. This was an order written and signed by the depositor asking the goldsmith (or banker) to pay the stated sum to the person named. An early example reads:

> Mr. Thomas Fowles.
>
> I desire you to pay unto Mr. Samuel Howard or order upon receipt hereof the sum of nine pounds thirteen shillings and sixe pence and place it to the account of yor servant
>
> Edmond Warcupp.
>
> 14 Augt. 1675.
>
> £9 13 6d.
>
> For Mr. Thomas Fowles, Gouldsmith at his shop between the two Temple gates, Fleete streete.

The early goldsmith-bankers found that large sums were left in their hands for long periods. It seemed a pity to let the money lie in the strong-boxes doing no good to anyone except the depositor. So they used these sums of money as loans or in other productive ways bringing in interest and other earnings. This was a safe proceeding as long as the money was not needed by the depositor unexpectedly. Some bankers guessed correctly how far they could go and what was the likelihood of the cash being wanted. Others were not so clever, or lucky, and when a number of depositors happened to want their money at the same time, found they were short of cash. So the bank would fail and the depositors lose their money. Numbers of small family banking businesses were established during the eighteenth century in country towns;

there were 230 of them in 1797. Those that were conducted with discretion developed into banking houses that have had a long history, and some survive to-day, though amalgamated with others into large banks. Some of the country banks were not run on sound lines; an element of gambling crept in. If rumours of a bank being unsound were spread about, or a general depression in trade threatened all business, most depositors might want to withdraw their money; a 'run on the bank' would follow and if the bank had insufficient funds in hand it would be obliged to close its doors. Bankruptcy followed, with the ruin of many people who had trusted their money to the bank.[1]

For the protection of the public it became necessary to legislate for the better conduct of banking. Most of the small family banks disappeared or were absorbed, until to-day the number of banks is comparatively small. The Big Five are familiar to us all.

PURCHASING POWER. We may not be personally interested in banks and the world of finance, but each of us is greatly concerned with the value of our money; this value is best measured by what money will buy. A penny went a long way when sweets were four ounces to the penny. The purchasing power of the penny was then much higher than it is now. Diagram XI shows how the purchasing power of the pound has declined since 1938. This should be compared with Diagram VIII (p. 23), which presents the same facts but from another angle.

We cannot here go into all the reasons for this decline. But if we are to understand the various methods being tried by governments in the many countries affected, as

[1] A vivid account of a crisis in the affairs of a country bank is given in Stanley Weyman's novel, *Ovington's Bank.*

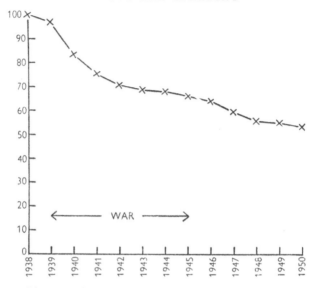

Diagram XI—Purchasing Power of Pound (1938=100)

we are, by a declining purchasing power (or, to put it the the other way, by a rising cost of living) we must study some of the underlying causes.

DEMAND AND SUPPLY. The purchasing power of money falls if the total volume of demand exceeds the total supplies. If the demand is greater than the supply, then more of such goods will be produced, and, as long as the demand is unsatisfied, prices, and the cost of living, will go up unless controlled in some way. This rise in prices is part of what is technically called 'inflation'. If, on the other hand, the supply of goods is greater than the demand, then the amount of goods produced will decrease as the falling prices may not make it worth while producing them.

The total volume of demand for everything depends on the total incomes that are being earned by all who are employed, and on the proportion of those incomes which are not actually spent, either because people save, or because the Government imposes taxation. It is very difficult to forecast exactly either the total of incomes or the amount that will be saved. The total of demand is thus always a matter of some uncertainty.

It is an even more difficult task for a producer to decide what the future demand for his particular goods may be. If there is likely to be a heavy demand, it is worth his while planning for greater production; if there is a declining demand, he may run the risk of having his goods left on his hands, or of having to sell them at a loss. There is no fool-proof method of doing this any more than there is of predicting what horse will win the Derby. Some goods, such as food, are in fairly steady demand, but others have to take their chance of changing fashions. Past experience is a useful guide, but human wants, likes, and dislikes are unpredictable. Hence there is always an element of speculation in industry and trade.

BOOMS AND SLUMPS. Periodically it seems that everyone makes bad forecasts; then, as a result and for other reasons, we get a general decline in trade, or a 'slump'. Diagram XII shows this very clearly for the period between 1929 and 1934. The years 1924 and 1925 were prosperous ones for trade; there was a 'boom'. The history of industry and trade seems to be an alternation of booms and slumps, and one problem our statesmen and economists have to face is how to avoid such violent ups and downs. It would clearly be better if the general level could be kept steady. A bad slump means increased unemployment (see Diagram XII) with all its distress

EARNING AND SPENDING

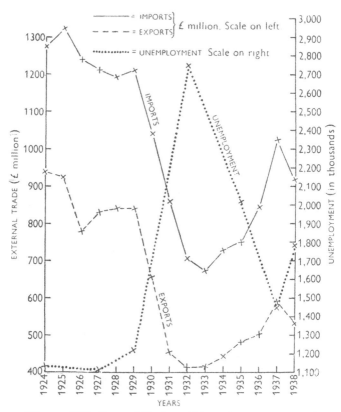

Diagram XII—External Trade and Unemployment, 1924-1938

and wastefulness. In 1932 there were nearly two and three-quarter million unemployed in this country. A slump also means that some producers, especially those working on a small scale and with small reserves, may be ruined. The whole country feels the effects of such a loss of production.

The modern policy of keeping industry and trade steady

84

without great fluctuations is known as 'full-employment'. Since the end of the war in 1945, Great Britain has been in a phase of full-employment, or even of excessive demand, and the main problems have been to prevent prices rising and the purchasing power of our money declining.

It can be seen that if we are to prevent prices rising we must either increase supplies or reduce demand. If we look at the various methods that have been adopted by governments (not only by our own) we can see that they fall into two groups; measures to increase supplies, and measures to limit demand.

INCREASING SUPPLIES. Among the measures to increase or improve supplies we find:

1. *Higher production.* This is the major problem that has to be faced. The Government has tried to secure that as many people as possible are employed productively, and that raw materials are imported in sufficient quantities to keep them fully employed.

2. *Reducing costs.* Prices can be lowered if the costs of production can be reduced. Much thought has been given to this problem in recent years. The aim is to avoid waste of materials, time and energy, by using up-to-date machinery and carefully organised methods in allocating work. The Government has encouraged this process by the Industrial Councils and Working Parties (see pp. 38, 40) and by arranging for representative managers and workers to tour other countries (such as the U.S.A.) to see how other manufacturers have dealt with similar problems.

3. *New factories, etc.* The Government helps by providing capital for expanding or re-equipping old factories, or for starting new ones.

4. *Controls of supplies and production.* This is done by allocating to industries quotas of raw materials according to Government plans. One purpose is to see that common needs are met first so that the supply of commodities meets the demand; this prevents manufacturers concentrating on the production of luxury goods, for which higher prices (and profits) are obtainable than for ordinary goods. It further ensures that production of goods we can sell abroad is maintained.

5. *Subsidies and price-regulation.* This method has been used extensively since the war but it is not a new device; between the wars, for instance, our Government paid subsidies to the coal industry, and some countries subsidised their shipping. Subsidies are now chiefly paid for food. Their purpose is partly to keep prices reasonable for the consumer, and partly to offer farmers steady prices for their produce and so encourage them to grow more crops and raise more cattle. The State pays the farmer the difference between those prices paid to him and the lower ones paid by the consumer. This money does not come from some secret hoard, but from the taxes we pay; by dividing the total cost amongst all of us, whatever each earns, each pays a small share instead of some paying much higher prices because they have more money, and others having to do with little, or having to go without, because they cannot afford such high prices. In 1948 the food subsidies amounted to nearly four shillings per head per week.

LIMITING DEMAND. Among the measures to limit demand we find:

1. *Savings drives.* Most governments, including our own, have tried to persuade people to save more and spend less for the time being, because if they save they will not

only have a reserve for use in emergencies, but will also be able to buy goods when the supply has increased and prices have come down.

2. *Taxation.* Several countries, including our own, have imposed heavier taxation than is needed to cover their own expenditure so as to add to the amount of saving available for the building of new factories, new houses, new schools and new hospitals and for other desirable improvements we want as a community.

3. *Restricting profits and dividends.* Our own Government has tried to restrict profits and to secure that a large part of any profits made are kept in the business and not distributed to the owners or shareholders to be spent.

4. *Wage stand-stills.* Our own Government has tried, in consultation with the Trade Unions, to secure that wages should not rise faster than output is increased. At first sight increases of wages seem an attractive method of off-setting the fall of purchasing power, since if we had more money we could buy more things at the higher prices. But the increased demand (unless there is a corresponding rise in production) would send prices up still more, so that, on balance, we should not benefit. Moreover this increased demand might decrease the amount of goods we can offer for foreign trade. Diagram VII illustrates how average wages in a number of important industries have risen since 1938 ; this should be compared with Diagrams VIII and XI. Note that we are not here concerned with the larger problem of a just wage, but only with the relation between wages and purchasing power.

All these methods are in a sense experiments and may be discarded if unsuccessful or if the condition of trade and industry permits. It may be necessary to try other methods.

We are living in a very different world from that of the nineteenth century and are therefore obliged to seek solutions to problems that did not worry the Victorians although problems existed that called for similar boldness in action. In their day there was widespread poverty and distress such as we can hardly imagine and should certainly find intolerable; our surprise is that our forebears could regard such social conditions with complacency. There were, however, some who were horrified at the conditions under which so many struggled to live, and they strove for reforms and for changes in policy. Their enlightened attitude has won the day. If we were indifferent to the conditions of living of others, we could return to the old policy of non-interference. We could reduce the cost of living drastically by reducing wages, but we can no longer be indifferent to social conditions, so we have to search for new ways of meeting such problems. The fact that our prosperity as a nation depends on trade with other countries is one that calls for closer study.

Subjects for inquiry and discussion

1. Find out the metal composition and value of a present-day shilling and of a penny.
2. Make a list of banks in your locality. Have any of them absorbed former banks ? If so, find out something of their history.
3. What were the advantages of the small country bank over our centralised system of a few big banks ?
4. Have a conversation with the oldest person you can meet about prices and wages when he (or she) was young.
5. Compare carefully Diagrams VII, VIII, and XI. What deductions do you make ?

6. Do you think that the simplest way of reducing the cost of living would be for the Government to issue an order for all prices to be reduced by, say ten per cent? What do you think would be the effect on producers and consumers ?

7. What is the Black Market ? What conditions are favourable to its existence ? How would you suppress it ?

8. Read the history of the Bank of England. (An encyclopædia article would suffice.) What was gained, and lost, by its nationalisation ?

9. Why is the forgery of currency notes and bank-notes such a serious crime ? Find out what precautions are taken to make forgery very difficult.

10. Why are wages in London sometimes paid at a higher rate than in other towns ? Give examples of this practice. Is it justified ?

CHAPTER 9

EXTERNAL TRADE

THIS country with its crowded population cannot live on its own resources. Robinson Crusoe could manage to do so on his island, but, even so, he found the carefully assorted salvage of the wrecked ship a welcome addition to the local produce. The arrival of Man Friday greatly increased the efficiency of the economy.

A few facts will show our dependence on commodities coming from other countries.

There are few raw materials of industry of which we have more than we need. Coal, china clay, and brick clay are among the rare examples of this.

We can produce only half of the food we eat. (See Diagram X). No possible extension of farming can entirely make up the other half. We must buy food from other countries.

Our country cannot supply us with such things as cotton, rubber, tea, and so on.

To get the things we need—if we are to go on living as we are accustomed—we must sell goods to other countries. This means that we must produce the things they want to buy.

The following list of Imports and Exports for 1947 is rather long, but a careful study of it will tell you much about our resources and our needs.

EXTERNAL TRADE

I. *Food, drink and tobacco*	*£million*
Total	805.4
A. Grain and flour	141.6
B. Feeding-stuffs for animals	14.5
C. Animals, living, for food	12.1
D. Meat	147.3
E. Dairy produce	124.5
F. Fresh fruit and vegetables	83.7
G. Beverages and cocoa preparations	88.7
H. Other food	145.6
I. Tobacco	47.4

II. *Raw materials and articles mainly manufactured*	
Total	559.8
B. Other non-metalliferous mining and quarry products	14.9
C. Iron ore and scrap ..	20.2
D. Non-ferrous metalliferous ores and scrap ..	24.2
E. Wood and timber ..	107.1
F. Raw cotton and cotton waste	58.8
G. Wool, raw and waste, and woollen rags	62.2
H. Silk, raw and waste, and artificial silk waste ..	2.2
I. Other textile materials	24.2
J. Seeds and nuts for oil, oils, fats, resins and gums ..	118.8
K. Hides and skins, undressed	39.9
L. Paper-making materials	27.3
M. Rubber	27.8
Other Class II ..	32.2

III. *Articles wholly or mainly manufactured*	
Total	399.4

I. *Food, drink and tobacco*	*£million*
Total	64.7
A. Grain and flour	1.8
D. Meat	0.5
E. Dairy produce	1.0
G. Beverages and cocoa preparations	19.5
H. Other food	23.2
I. Tobacco	18.7

II. *Raw materials and articles mainly manufactured* ..	
Total	34.2
A. Coal	2.5
B. Other non-metalliferous mining and quarry products	2.0
D. Non-ferrous metalliferous ores and scrap ..	10.7
G. Wool, raw and waste, and woollen rags	7.4
J. Seeds and nuts for oil, oils, fats, resins and gums ..	1.4
K. Hides and skins, undressed	1.2
L. Paper-making materials	0.3
Other Class II	8.7

III. *Articles wholly or mainly manufactured*	
Total	998.9
A. Coke and manufactured fuel	0.2
B. Pottery, glass, abrasives, etc.	32.9
C. Iron and steel and manufactures thereof ..	84.3
D. Non-ferrous metals and manufactures thereof	40.4
E. Cutlery, hardware, implements and instruments	35.3

Note : *The capital letters at the beginnings of the entries under ' Imports ' correspond to those under ' Exports ' and vice versa.*

IMPORTS—		EXPORTS—	
B. Pottery, glass, abrasives, etc.	6.4	F. Electrical goods and apparatus	49.4
C. Iron and steel and manufactures thereof	15.0	G. Machinery	180.6
D. Non-ferrous metals and manufactures thereof	79.3	H. Manufactures of wood and timber	1.5
E. Cutlery, hardware, implements and instruments	5.1	I. Cotton yarns and manufactures	77.7
F. Electrical goods and apparatus	2.3	J. Woollen and worsted yarns and manufactures	57.9
G. Machinery	29.6	K. Silk and artificial silk yarns and manufactures	29.5
H. Manufactures of wood and timber	16.9	L. Manufactures of other textile materials	28.0
I. Cotton yarns and manufactures	17.4	M. Apparel	31.7
L. Manufactures of other textile materials	15.9	N. Footwear	6.7
M. Apparel	3.4	O. Chemicals, drugs, dyes and colours	67.4
O. Chemicals, drugs, dyes and colours	26.7	P. Oils, fats and resins, manufactured	8.2
P. Oils, fats and resins, manufactured	92.4	Q. Leather and manufactures thereof	7.0
Q. Leather and manufactures thereof	·15.7	R. Paper, cardboard, etc.	17.2
R. Paper, cardboard, etc.	21.7	S. Vehicles (including locomotives, ships and aircraft)	168.1
S. Vehicles (including locomotives, ships and aircraft)	6.0	T. Rubber manufactures	6.3
Other Class III	45.6	U. Miscellaneous articles wholly or mainly manufactured	68.6
IV. *Animals not for food*	7.7	IV. *Animals not for food*	3.6
V. *Parcel post*	15.1	V. *Parcel post*	35.7

Note : *The capital letters at the beginnings of the entries under ' Imports ' correspond to those under ' Exports ' and vice versa.*

The next point to examine is what countries trade with us and to what extent they are willing to exchange goods with us. The following list gives the countries and also the value (in £million) of what we buy from them (imports) and what we sell to them (exports).

1947				IMPORTS FROM	EXPORTS TO
Argentine Republic		..	..	130.7	34.7
Australia	..	..	..	97.1	71.8
Belgium	..	..	..	35.5	33.6
Brazil	..	..	..	23.6	17.2
Burma	..	..	..	3.6	20.2
Canada	..	..	..	230.3	43.4
Ceylon	..	..	..	22.6	11.5
Denmark	..	..	..	27.1	26.2
Dutch East Indies	..	..	..	1.0	5.5
Dutch West Indies		..	..	34.8	2.8
Egypt	..	..	..	14.8	22.0
Eire	..	..	..	35.2	55.9
Finland	..	..	..	29.3	9.9
France	..	..	..	31.4	23.6
Germany (and Austria)		..	..	20.0	21.1
India, Pakistan etc.		..	..	94.4	91.6
Malaya (British)	..	..	..	29.8	30.1
Netherlands	..	..	..	26.2	30.8
New Zealand	..	..	..	89.6	43.1
Nigeria	..	..	..	36.1	15.4
Northern Rhodesia		..	..	15.6	2.0
Soviet Union	..	..	..	7.5	12.3
Sweden	..	..	..	41.1	29.9
United States of America			..	294.9	47.9
Union of South Africa		..	..	25.4	91.8
		TOTAL	..	1,787.5	1,137.1
British countries	..	..	..	806.3	599.6
Foreign countries	..	..	..	981.2	537.5

A general picture of the values of imports and exports from 1924 to 1938 is given in Diagram XII. It will be noticed that the imports and exports curves follow similar courses.

With these two lists and the diagram before us for reference we can now proceed with our study of external trade.

External trade is governed by the same conditions of supply and demand as trade amongst ourselves, but there are some special considerations to be taken into account.

BALANCE OF PAYMENTS. An important point to note about external trade is that we have to pay for what we buy. This seems an obvious and even childish thing to put in words, but it is of first importance. Put in another way, the goods and services we sell to foreign countries have to pay for what we buy from them; payments must be balanced.

Diagram XII gives the impression that over the period there represented the account never was balanced; the interval or gap between imports and exports in 1926, for instance, was considerable. How then was the difference made up? Part of the answer is covered by the term 'invisible exports'. Our ships earn money for us by carrying goods and passengers; the figures for imports include the cost of bringing them here; in many cases this is done by British ships. The figures for exports show their value at a British port; in many cases we earn also the freights of carrying them to their destinations. Our insurance companies and banks render services to customers in other countries. These and other services are not recorded in our trade returns but they help to balance the account.

INVESTMENTS. There was before the Second World War another very large item in the account—investments in other countries by people in this country. Thus a country, let us call it Pneumania, may have wanted a railway and decided to buy the necessary locomotives, coaches, rails, etc., in this country, and employ British engineers. Pneumania raised a loan in London; provided it seemed sound and the terms were sufficiently attractive, the loan was taken up by the public and the banks. Pneumania had to pay interest on that loan, and this came to this country in the form of goods. Investments of this kind lay up for us claims in other countries; in time of war such claims can be realised in the form of goods urgently needed. That is what happened in both world wars, but

94

in the second the need was so great that we realised a large
part of such investments, particularly those in America;
this has meant the loss of one method by which the trading
account was balanced. We no longer have that to fall back
on; hence the frequency with which we hear of the 'gap'.

STERLING AREA. There is, however, another difficulty.
Some countries do their trading in sterling (see p. 78),
which is our currency, but other countries trade in dollars
(the U.S.A. currency.) The sterling area (as it is called)
includes the Commonwealth countries (*but not Canada*)
and other parts of the Empire, with the addition of two
or three other small countries. When we want to buy
cotton or tobacco from the U.S.A. or wheat from Canada
we have to use dollars, and we cannot earn those unless
they want the goods we have to sell. The problem of
trade with the U.S.A. is that most of our products are
also produced in that country and our manufacturers
have to persuade them to buy our goods.

If you now look at the list on page 93 and compare the
figures for imports and exports for each country, you will
see that in some cases, e.g. Belgium, they are close together
in value, but others, e.g. Canada, are far apart. It was
possible to have such gaps in the accounts in 1947 because,
as a temporary help, the U.S.A. under its European
Recovery Programme provided the necessary dollars
(Marshall Aid). Whether in the long run we shall succeed in increasing permanently our sales of goods to
Canada and the U.S.A. only time will show. It must,
however, be remembered that the U.S.A. wants to sell its
products, and if we cannot buy, there is no trade between
us. At times we have had to cut down, for instance, our
purchases of petrol and tobacco; this hits the producer
in the U.S.A. (as well as our motorists and smokers) just

as much as we are hit when our goods are refused. Trade is a reciprocal business; one country cannot trade all by itself, and one of the world problems is how to restore open trading conditions between all countries.

The Government controls external trade by means of licences, quotas, etc. for the import and export of goods. Many factors have to be taken into consideration, such as, what goods we need most, what goods we can sell to other countries, what we can afford to buy, and so on. Decisions on such matters call for considerable knowledge of facts and careful judgment. In this way it is possible to ensure that our resources are not wasted but used to the best advantage. We naturally chafe at the restrictions and regulations with all the paper-work involved, but one thing is clear, unless we work according to some well thought-out scheme we may find ourselves short of food and raw materials.

We are indeed going through one of those periods of great social and economic change, such as the Tudor period and the Industrial Revolution were, to which it is difficult to adjust established habits and ways of thinking. Such changes are not deliberately brought about by Government policy; they are the result of many factors over which there can be little control. Now we are trying to avoid the mistakes of the past, as in the Industrial Revolution, when the devil took the hindmost, by regulating, as far as possible, the rate of the change and its nature. It is certainly an interesting and even exciting period in which to live.

TARIFFS. Governments have in the past regulated trade, but not on the present scale. Treaties and agreements between nations have always been a means of fostering trade. Customs duties have been levied on imports sometimes for the sake of revenue, and at other times in order to protect a home industry by preventing too great an influx of goods which would compete with our own. In the Commonwealth and Empire we have helped each other by favourable tariffs. Now that our period of Free Trade is past and customs duties and other limitations are in force, the smuggler has returned, bringing with him his unattractive colleague the black marketeer; they seem less romantic figures than their predecessors.

Sometimes in order to sell our goods to other countries we have to take in exchange goods we do not really want; this is a thorny problem and can only be overcome when countries, or groups of countries, pool their resources and distribute them according to need. Preliminary steps have been taken towards such a desirable end; the countries in West Europe, for instance, are reviewing their common economic problems in the hope of easing the situation in which we all find ourselves. Already some adjustments in tariffs have been made; they may seem small at present, but there is every reason to hope that further progress will be made in this direction. Then there is the International Trade Organisation (under the United Nations Organisation), which brings together over fifty countries to discuss ways and means of lowering trade barriers between nations. A General Agreement was signed in 1947 by twenty-three countries (covering three-quarters of world trade); this has resulted in tariff reductions. A further series of negotiations in 1949 was joined by eleven additional countries. So step by step the nations move towards a sounder world economy. But centuries-old traditions, the spirit of nationalism, the greediness of some merchants and the selfishness of most of us stand in the way of rapid agreement.

Meanwhile we must continue to wrestle with the problem of reaching a satisfactory balance of our external trade and so promote our general industrial prosperity.

Subjects for inquiry and discussion

1. Study the list of imports and exports on pages 91-2.
    (i) What items under imports are not to be found under exports? And exports that are not imports?
    (ii) Make lists of (a) the six largest imports,
                        (b) the six largest exports.
    (iii) What bearing has the list of imports on the building of houses?
    (iv) Why should the Parcel Post be included?
2. Study the list of countries on page 93.
    (i) Rearrange the lists in the order of values of imports and exports.
    (ii) Make a list of those countries where imports and exports are fairly balanced.
    (iii) Pick out the six countries with which there is the greatest disparity between imports and exports. Can you account for this?
3. Make a list of ten common foods we eat. Where do they come from?
4. Study Diagram XII.
    (i) In what year was the gap between imports and exports (a) at its greatest and (b) at its narrowest?
    (ii) What connexion is shown between unemployment and external trade?
5. Why is inflation regarded with such alarm?
6. Make a list of the years during the past century in which there were booms or slumps. An economic history will supply the information.
7. Construct a diagram similar to Diagram XII for the years since 1945.

8. State the case for and against a big cut in our tobacco imports from the U.S.A.
9. What is the purpose of advertising? Ask some of your friends if they have been influenced in their purchases by advertisements. In 1935 about eighty million pounds was spent on advertising in the U.K. Would it be wise to reduce costs by reducing the amount of advertising?
10. It has been said that if every inhabitant of China bought one pocket-handkerchief from Great Britain, our cotton industry would flourish as never before. What other undeveloped markets can we hope to enter?
11. Study what is being done to develop industry in, and trade with, our Colonial Empire.
12. Find out what progress has been made towards a freer state of trade in (a) Western Europe and (b) amongst the member countries of the United Nations Organisation.

INDEX

Agricultural Co-operative Managers' Association, 74
Agricultural Wages Acts (1924, 1940), 20
Amalgamated Engineering Union, 32
Amalgamated Society of Engineers, 32
Apprenticeship, 18
Arbitration, 41
  Board of, 42
  Court of, 38
Assembly line, 46

Balance of payments, 93-4
Balance of trade, 58
Bank of England, 79
Bank-note, 79
Banks, 51, 80-1
Barter, 77
Birth rate, 2
Black-coated worker, 15
Boom, 83
B.B.C., 62
British Employers' Confederation, 35
British Medical Association, 27
Building Societies, 12, 51-2
Burnham Committee, 39
Burying in Woollen Acts (1666, 1678), 57

Capital, 47, 85
Cartel, 53-4
Catering Wages Act (1943), 20
Census, 1
Chain Store, 70
Cheque, 79
Civil Service, 17
Classes, 9, 14
Closed shop, 34
Coal, 63
Combination Acts, (1799, 1800), 28
  Repeal Acts (1824, 1825), 29
Committee of Investigation, 43

Conciliation Board, 39; officer, 42
Contract out, or in, 30
Conveyor belt, 46
Co-operative Society, 53, 71-2
  Agricultural, 73
  Producers', 73
  Wholesale, 72-3
Co-partnership, 53
Cost of living, 22
Costs, reducing, 85
Court of Enquiry, 42
Currency Note, 79

Death rate, 2
Debenture, 51
Demand and supply, 82
Demand, limiting, 86
Department Store, 70
Dividend, 50
Dollar, 95

Emergency Powers Act (1939), 43
Emigration, 6
Employment Exchange, 25
Employers' Associations, 35
Engineering & Allied Employers' National Federation, 35
European Recovery Programme, 95

Family allowances, 59
Federation of British Industries, 35
Food, 66-7, 90
Free Trade, 97
Friendly Society, 29
Full employment, 84

Goldsmith-banker, 80
Grand National Consolidated Trades Union (1832), 32

Help-yourself Stores, 71
Herts. & Beds. Co-operative Bacon Factory, 74
Holidays with Pay Act (1938) 42
Home production, 67

INDEX

Imports and exports, 91-3
Industrial Courts Act (1919), 42
Industrial Revolution, 7, 11, 28, 96
Inflation, 82
International Trade Organisation, 97
Investment abroad, 94
Invisible export, 94
Iron & Steel Corporation, 63

Joint Industrial Council, 38-9
Joint Production Committee, 40
Joint Stock Company, 50

Labour, division of, 46
  Skilled and unskilled, 14
Labour Exchanges, 25
Labour, Ministry of, 37-8, 41-3
Laissez-faire, 58
Limited Liability Company, 50

Management Advisory Committee, 40
Manufactures, 17
Market, 69
Marshall Aid, 95
Mass-production, 45
Middleman, 68
Money, 77-8
Monopoly, 54
Motor Trade Association, 35
Multiple Store, 70
National Arbitration Tribunal, 42
National Farmers' Union, 74
National Association of Trade Unions (1845), 32
National Insurance, 24, 27, 59
National Union of Teachers, 35
National Whitley Council, 39
Nationalisation, 60
Navigation Act (1672), 57

Occupations, 26
Overtime, 21

Partnership, 48
PAYE, 24
Piece-work, 21
Ploughing back, 51

Population, density, 5
  distribution, 7
  growth, 2
Post Office, 60
Preference share, 51
Price regulation, 86
Production, 85
Profession, 14
Profit, restricting, 87
  undistributed, 50
Profit-sharing, 53
Public Assistance, 25
Public Corporation, 61
Public Utility Services, 60
Purchasing power, 81

Restrictive practices, 33
Road Haulage Act (1938), 20
Road Traffic Act (1930), 42

Saving, 48, 86
Shareholder, 49, 52
Share, 52
  kinds of, 50-1
Shift, 21
Shop, independent, 69
Silver penny, 78
Sliding scale, 23
Slump, 83
Socialism, 59
Southern Counties Agricultural Trading Society, 74
Standardisation, 46
Statute of Artificers (1563), 19
Sterling, 78;
  area, 95
Stock, 52
Stock Exchange, 52
Store, kinds of, 70
Strike, 37, 40
  Dock (1949), 43
Subsidy, 86
Sweating, 20

Tariff, 96
Taxation, 86
Trade, wholesale and retail, 68
Trade Boards Act (1919), 20

INDEX

Trade Unions, 19
  Acts (1871-1946), 30
  closed shop, 34
  defined, 27
  functions, 32
  history, 27
  membership, 31
  organisation, 33
  political fund, 30
Trades Union Congress, 27, 34
Transport & General Workers'
  Union, 41
Trusts, 53-4

Unemployment, 83-4

Wages, calculating, 21
  Council, 20
  fixing, 19
  standstill, 87
Wall Street, 53
White-collar, 15
Whitley Committee, 38
Wiltshire Farmers, 74
Woolworths, 70
Working Parties, 40
Works Committee, 38, 39, 47

For EU product safety concerns, contact us at Calle de José Abascal, 56–1°, 28003 Madrid, Spain or eugpsr@cambridge.org.

www.ingramcontent.com/pod-product-compliance
Ingram Content Group UK Ltd.
Pitfield, Milton Keynes, MK11 3LW, UK
UKHW042209180425
457623UK00011B/113